The Priestess of Mokhi Maya

A Love Story

A Messianic Invocation

We are gathered to seek the Way, the Truth, the Life
To open the channels of Spirit by way of One Who became the Truth
That we may more perfectly worship the embodiment of Grace that
He is; That we may become;
That we may unify our consciousness with Him;
That, in the act of seeking, as attunement comes, we may learn to be
    centered, selflessly, within the Will of God;
That, as the events of the Great Days draw near, we may recognize
    from whence they come and we may serve;
That we may better understand the next obvious step in the evolu-
    tion of the soul in the earth;
That the Holy Purpose be ever more deeply instilled within us;
That the seed that is Christ within each one may grow to deliver the
    Messiah unto the earth:
We seek the Truth as it may be given here and now.

Author's Note: This is a prayer written by the channel that she
sometimes used to prepare herself for contact with the Source
when the readings first began.

"To the Children of the Light"
©

The Priestess of Mokhi Maya

A Love Story

Dr. Dennis L. Hunter

Credits:
Cover Design: Barbara A. Swanson, Pica² Graphics, Colorado Springs, CO
Photography: Dennis L. Hunter, Grand Junction, CO
Text Design and Composition: Barbara A. Swanson, Pica² Graphics
Editor and Project Manager: Sharon Green, Panache Editorial, Inc. Colorado Springs, CO
Printed by: Technical Communication Services, North Kansas City, MO

ISBN: 978-0-9748650-1-0

Author's Disclaimer

This shall not be the complete and actual story of the Priestess of Mokhi Maya, but rather the best recollections of one person's experience with the Priestess. The possibilities and implications of the true essence of this magnificent soul are far too expansive to be adequately covered in one small book from one person's memory. There are those from this time as well as other times and places who have had their own experiences with the Priestess.

Editors and Publishers are often more comfortable in guiding authors to represent material such as this as fiction, or at best, "based upon a true story." Although there may be some poetic license and distortion from the fog of personal subjective prejudice, great care has been taken to ensure that every word of this story is true; to the best of the author's ability to relate it. This is a chronicle about real people, events and places. However, if there are those who are more comfortable with other interpretations that is their prerogative.

Published by
Sacred Mountain Publishers
P.O. Box 3042
Grand Junction, Colorado 81502

For information regarding psychic readings mentioned in this book,
view the Website at
www.readingsfromthesource.com

Dedicated to Kayla Susanna

So that you might remember your Grandmother

Contents

Prologue

I know what lust is. I know what infatuation is. And, I know what love is. But, this was something very different. It was something primal, sublime, and eternal.

I can't remember a time when I did not know her. She is an inseparable part of me that lives in the depths of my being. Her spirit is the essential breath that feeds and nourishes my soul. Whether I understand it or not, or whether I know it or not; she has always been there. She is the essence of purpose, beauty, and grace.

She is born of unwavering compassion and relentless commitment. She is a door through which a multi-verse of unseen worlds are created, collide, and fulfill their destiny. She is that always familiar, comforting presence; that one precious treasure that emerges over and over again, beckoning throughout the many times and the many places. She is not just a part of creation, but the reason that creation exists.

She is the rock upon which the hardened heart is broken, healed, and allowed to flourish once more.

Before her countenance the sacred scriptures of all the ages are silenced, returned to dust, mournfully awaiting their resurrection which can only come through the magic of her divine sagas. Without her, the gates through which messiahs and saviors beckon remain tightly shut. Without her, all of heaven's wonders remain unfulfilled; the universe lies still and barren. Without her, death rules eternally; and, there is no resurrection.

Thus is the nature of that one supreme Goddess that dwells both within and without …

Chapter 1

When First We Met

The drive had been tedious and exhausting. I was still under the hypnotic spell of the highway's flickering white line, as I collapsed into the soft cushion of a creaking wicker chair. There was a slight chill to the heavy, humid air wafting through the lobby. The scent of an unfamiliar, musty brine teased my nostrils. Through the screened windows I could hear the pulsing waves of the Atlantic, relentlessly pounding upon shores that seemed replete with unquestioning surrender.

The waves were echoing a halcyon murmur, somehow reverberating from a forgotten chamber within a calcified soul. Relaxing more deeply into the chair, I closed my eyes and began to merge into the mesmerizing ebb and flow of restless waves that seemed to mock my labored breathing. Succumbing to the monotonous lullaby I was soon released into welcomed sleep.

Some time later, I was aroused back to consciousness by the measured clacking of hollow-sounding footsteps, pounding across a tiled floor. Taking a long ragged breath and peering through awakening eyes, I observed a sophisticated young woman emerging out of a long, darkened hallway. As she strode into the room, I was immediately captivated by the regal countenance that can only come from a woman alive with the presence of the creator. A stunning, dark maroon cape was draped around her shoulders, reaching almost to her knees. Like most arriving visitors, she wished to make contact with the ocean.

She stared into the torrent, acknowledging the moon's glow, and bore witness to the lunging of the waves. Through the silvery light, I could see her visage with long cascading hair sensuously caressing the sides of her face, neck and shoulders. After a moment she abruptly turned, thus shattering her wistful communion.

Almost as if by an explosion, her startled eyes collided with mine. There was a beauty and a grace in those eyes that a man could willingly become lost in. She had been unaware of my presence. But now there was a riveting connection between us. I wondered if I had not seen this one somewhere before. The instant in which we lingered was etched into a place within my soul where memory embraces eternity.

Smiling knowingly, she turned smartly and disappeared into the darkened hallway from which she had come. As she faded from view, I remembered thinking how fortunate a man might be to have one such as this as his life companion.

Her friend, whom I would later know as Alexis, arrived an instant later. She was a bit harried, replete with a head full of the considerable challenges of securing last minute accommodations at a major seaside resort. Exuding a strained sigh of frustration she muttered something about trying to get everyone in the same place at the same time. Stomping through the lobby, she left almost as soon as she had arrived.

A while later my inner musings were interrupted by the sound of a familiar voice calling my name. I hadn't seen Turner since we shared room 119 in Old Main dormitory at Northern Arizona University in the fall of 1969. He met a young lady while going to school in Flagstaff; became engaged, and followed her home to New York City, hoping to launch a career in the infant field of computer programming. He was a tall, wiry lad with a weakened, clumsy leg that never fully recovered from polio. People often saw him as having the look and demeanor of a Baptist evangelist. At one time, he actually did participate in the ministry.

It was clear that he was a godly man; very devout, a sincere seeker of mystical insights and transcendent truths. Even at that time, his knowledge and actual experience with things of a spiritual nature were rather astonishing and intricate. He also had a tendency to tout a rather playful sense of humor, which was laced with an innocent humility that I found unique and refreshing.

It was by complete coincidence that Fred and I arrived in Virginia Beach at the same time. He had spontaneously driven down from New York with several friends in order to attend a short weekend conference at the Association for Research & Enlightenment. We usually just called it the "A. R. E."

It was the administrative and educational center for the renowned psychic, channel and seer, Edgar Cayce. With a little help from the sixties generation his fame was rapidly spreading across the burgeoning new-age culture. Turner and I, being enthralled by the information, had started an Edgar Cayce study group while attending the university in Flagstaff.

I had just arrived from Arizona, having decided to spend some quality postgraduate time in Virginia Beach. I figured that it would not be a problem finding seasonal employment, and looked forward to the opportunity to further scrutinize "the readings" as they were called. It was also a good time to commune with the ocean while contemplating the moral implications of accepting a draft notice for military service.

I had spent the previous summer in Virginia Beach working in the kitchen and grounds of the Marshal's, the ocean-side resort where many Cayce-inspired visitors would come to vacation and attend conferences. It was a good place to meet and scrutinize some of the more popular mystics and esoteric authors of the time. This was in an era when sleeping (channeling) prophets and knowledge of previous lives was not very mainstream. It was not always easy to find folks open to or even interested in hearing about such irrational and heretical nonsense.

At that time, it was still possible for the general public to simply walk into the A. R. E. library and conduct personal research on thousands of Cayce channeled readings. My mind was rampant with an unending multitude of questions.

After some transitory musing about the coincidence of our meeting, we realized that neither of us had made any plans for accommodations. Woody, Fred's freshly minted nickname, said that the friends he had driven down with were also looking for lodging.

He invited me to join his party. I had initially supposed that I would simply sleep in my car or on the beach while I secured a summer job and more permanent housing. Woody indicated they were pooling their money in order to secure a modest motel room. After the long drive from Arizona the thought of a hot shower became immediately irresistible. And it was a lot easier than dodging the local constable.

Being a destination resort, a room would cost a small fortune. But there was a plan. We would put the mattresses on the floor, if necessary, so that there would be plenty of bed space. We reasoned that if one included the not-so-comfortable box springs, there should be room for all. Sounded like a good idea so the deal was made. I was all in.

After a refreshing walk on the beach, Woody came back to once more find me in the front lobby. He announced that "the girls" had found something down toward the 17th Street Pier. It turned out that his friends were all female. Imagine, young people, single, being of the opposite sex, sharing a motel room without a chaperone! How shocking! Even though it was already 1970, it still sounded a bit risqué.

I mused for a moment as this was the precise attitude that resulted in my turning down a chance to join some "free spirits" during my previous pilgrimage to Virginia. They were on their way to what turned out to be the legendary open-air concert in a farmer's field that we would all come to know as Woodstock.

Woody was a person of impeccable character. His offer remained. The idea was intriguing and had some obvious merits. He explained that he and "the girls" were good friends and that they attended the same Cayce-styled "Search for God Study Group." Everything would be fine.

Late in the night, tired and exhausted, I dragged my backpack up the stairs as Woody showed me the place where I could get some much needed rest. As I arrived, Woody made the introductions, except for the one who was languishing in the shower. She seemed to take forever. I was finding that very annoying. Finally, the door opened and she stepped into the room, and lighted up with that same knowing smile. It was the same long-haired, maroon-caped lady I had encountered in the front lobby of the Marshal's, the inn at the edge of the sea.

It was the chance meeting of a lifetime. We talked long into the night. She offered and I accepted a massage that I shall never forget. We fell asleep in one another's arms. It was a sleep of profound bliss, a sleep of sublime innocence. As she lay with her head upon my shoulder, I could feel the ebb and flow of her sweet breath on my chest. It reminded me of the pulsing of the sea, foreshadowing the re-emergence of ancient passions.

When I awoke, Woody and his friends were gone, off to their Cayce conference, and then back to New York. The next day, I immediately found employment and more suitable lodging. When fall came, I prepared for military induction. After much soul-searching, I responded to my draft notification by enlisting. I was on my way to Fort Jackson, South Carolina and then on to Fort Benning, Georgia. This was not to be a time for romance.

Chapter 2

The Wedding

A bout a year later, Woody asked me to be his best man. I immediately accepted. I had never been to New York City. Fortunately, the timing was perfect and I was able to get an adequate furlough. This would be an exciting experience for a young air-cavalry trooper from Fort Hood, Texas; quite an adventure for a lad who had grown up in a Colorado mining town with a population of less than five hundred.

So, with a rush of excitement, I purchased some suitable civilian clothes and was off to what some simply called "The City." This was a time when you could just show up at any major airport and, for about fifty dollars, fly clear across the county on military standby. It was a cloudy, wet day. I watched through the small elliptical window of the plane as we broke through dark, heavy fog witnessing first-hand a familiar skyline that I had previously only seen in movies.

Emerging from the plane, I felt like I had just landed on another planet. The air was thick and damp, full of unpleasant odors; full of rumbling, clattering, buzzing sounds interrupted by the occasional wailing of emergency service vehicles. People's faces looked pasty white and ghoulish. They ran back and forth in massive packs pretending not to see one another. When purchasing some fast food, no one looked me in the eye. Change was not placed in my hand, but haphazardly tossed on the counter.

I fought a compassionate calling to tell these people that they didn't have to live this way. I had to stifle the compulsion to simply grab them by the shoulders and shake them; make them look me in the eye, so they could be awakened from their slumber. They could obviously escape by following the route that I had come, but in reverse.

To my surprise and great amusement, I soon discovered that many of these people actually believed that they lived in a very special place and that anyone of insight and value would really prefer to live in "The City" if they could only "make it" there. I found myself wondering out loud how many hopeful immigrants had set out to find the New World, but instead had become mired in this city, never really completing the journey and discovering the real America.

During my stay I came to realize that there was a prevalent attitudinal posture that rather arrogantly assumed that there was really nothing of much value outside of the walls of this coveted city-state. I even talked with a well-meaning individual who questioned if there were any paved roads or streetlights "out west" and whether or not it was possible to get books, or if they all had to be mail ordered. It took me a little while to realize that she was actually serious.

As the years passed, I have hopefully matured and become a little more insightful. Now, when in wilderness, I sometimes throw myself to the ground with great gratitude and supplication to whatever god that there may be that there is such a multitude of these well-meaning but woefully misguided individuals trapped in cities. Otherwise, much of the lands and sacred places that I treasure would be even more overrun, perhaps to the point of irrevocable desecration.

I sometimes wish even more people would prefer the allure of the crowded, noisy, narcissistic city and allow those of us who have become an endangered species to just languish a little longer within the fading miracle of pristine wilderness. I know and accept that change is inevitable, but that doesn't stop me from trying to search out the places where the cancerous madness has not yet quite encroached.

Okay, so I am getting a little carried away. And yes, I admit it. I can be a bit melodramatic. It is quite obvious that I don't feel comfortable in large urban centers. All that is true; but still, this was my first impression of this place where it seemed that "civilization" had gone amuck. And remember, this was what it felt like to someone who was well adapted to the monotonous regimentation and crowded quarters of the rather austere culture of a military post.

Swimming through the crowd I soon discovered a beaming smile belonging to friend Woody. I was rescued. Abruptly taking me in tow, he somehow got us to "the trains." He was living in a place he called the upper Bronx and seemed to be quite proud of his good fortune at finding an "affordable" apartment.

There was much news to catch up on. But we had to curtail our excited conversations during the rude intrusions from frenzied crowds that seemed to flow through the streets like the spring runoff of raging white water pulsing through the Grand Canyon.

We finally arrived at Woody's place. It was rather like a large closet with a bathroom at one end, not what I would call an apartment. If I remember clearly, it had a sort of efficiency kitchen in the opposite corner. The whole thing wasn't much bigger than a Virginia Beach motel room. The rent on this "affordable" apartment was enough to make payments on a good sized single-family home back in the real world.

And, we had to be careful. The landlord, who also resided within this old, rambling maze of a building, was suspicious of visitors. The plan was that I would stay with Woody right up to the wedding. I would then return for a final night's lodging in his "apartment" before returning to my post in Texas.

From my military training I was pretty good at land navigation. However, I knew it might be a challenge to find my way back to the airport upon conclusion of his nuptial festivities. Seeing my plight and demonstrating his usual tact, Woody grinned and suggested that he might be able to find someone to "help a lost soldier find his way home."

The next day we went to the half-completed World Trade Center. Woody showed me a project that had to do with the computerized drafting of a plan for a massive oil tanker. The apparatus was quite impressive for the time. Flailing about were several mechanical arms oozing tiny threads of brightly colored ink. They would hysterically swing about, bob up and down, abruptly starting, stopping, and starting again. Huge sheets of snow-white paper, the size of a small kitchen table, passively rolled along capturing with great precision and detail the plans for a ship that would safely and efficiently carry crude oil halfway around the world.

I don't recall which tower we were in, but I found it rather fascinating that while we were meandering about this stadium-sized office, other floors above us were still under construction. I remember buying a can of soda from a vending machine for the outrageous sum of twenty-five cents, the most I had ever spent on a can of Coke. I remember meticulously removing the ingenious pull-top tab and noisily slurping up the half frozen, icy foam as it erupted from the can.

I had sold my car prior to military induction in order to settle up some bills. I had been saving just about every penny of my Army pay to fund this trip. But, now was the time to splurge. I found it fascinating how you can take something for granted, then it can become a coveted delicacy when you don't have it for awhile—even a common can of soda.

High above the concrete-gray city, in a half-completed building, I was peering through a water-spotted window across the mighty Atlantic. I found myself wondering about the incredible vision and intestinal fortitude of the people who could conceive of such a structure and actively see it through to completion. I wondered how long it might be expected to stand. For a moment there was the sensation that the floor might be shifting beneath my feet.

Woody explained that the building was constructed so that it could gently sway back and forth, remaining flexible, yet dynamically resistant to gale-force winds or even mild earthquakes. He further explained that people were moving in and out of these dual megaliths in alternating shifts, because it would not be possible to get all the people in or out of the building at the same time. Some had even mused that it could become a self-contained city of close to thirty thousand inhabitants; complete within itself.

After tending to Woody's professional responsibilities we arrived at a small, experimental outpost of the Edgar Cayce Foundation where a branch of the Association for Research & Enlightenment was housed. Woody deposited me there while he continued on to complete some additional personal errands.

"The Center," as they called it, sported an excruciatingly small office with some dreary meeting rooms next to what was referred to as the bookstore. It was rather creatively squeezed into one corner of the awkwardly designed little complex. It all made me feel exceedingly claustrophobic, but then the whole city made me feel claustrophobic. However, this obscure little Mecca featured information on Edgar Cayce and also offered a treasure trove of other so called new-age books and publications. Many were quite controversial for the time and hard to find.

I found myself standing before an antique window whose distorted glass offered an out-of-focus view of the scurrying humanity in the street below. It was as if I were looking down into a narrow canyon formed by a collective collision of motley old buildings that desperately clung to opposing sides of an abyss.

It reminded me of the canyons of my childhood where my father would take us prospecting for gold, silver, molybdenum, or perhaps uranium ore. To me those were sacred canyons that would sometimes become caught up in the throes of magical sunsets blazing forth with hues of gold, crimson, and violet, gently caressing the edges of yawning shadows cast by meticulously sculpted walls that had survived all that the ravages of time had demanded of them.

As I stood there in contemplation, I began to sense a nourishing stillness. I felt a gentle and familiar presence. I became aware that someone was standing behind me, just to my left. Stepping forward, she placed her head on my shoulder and her arm around my waist. As we gazed out the window together, she gently whispered, "It is so good to see you again."

We both knew that something very special was on the horizon.

Susan explained that one day while visiting the Center, she noticed that no one was tending the incessant ringing of an all-but-abandoned telephone. People were wandering in and out looking rather perplexed with no helpful answers to their questions. So she picked up the phone and began taking messages, while simultaneously playing hostess and even selling a few books. By the end of the day, the overwhelmed director offered her a job and she graciously accepted. I would later discover that this was Susan's usual way of attracting employment.

Although temporary, it was a welcomed change from her hectic and erratic life as an off-Broadway costume designer. She had also formed a designer clothing business in one room of her mother's apartment with the assistance of a couple of friends. Later, it became quite lucrative to sell her fashion ideas, in the form of sketches, to some of the more established designers. Once she even worked with a subcontractor for a fledgling children's show which eventually became known as Sesame Street; but all that was a very long time ago.

The Center had become a meeting place where, while browsing for a new book, you might happen to bump into some of the most popular mystics and teachers of the era. She explained that there was always an abundance of friendly faces with whom you could freely indulge in your latest esoteric fantasies and insights with minimal concern for ridicule or rejection. The Center had become a much coveted safe house for a generation of budding new-age mystics.

There were occasional lectures and, of course, Edgar Cayce "Search for God" meetings. When Woody returned, I was introduced to an impromptu group of these proselytizing, young Cayce enthusiasts. As was the custom, participants would most often read excerpts from the catechism-like books on various subjects that offered up intermittent quotes from the Cayce material. The idea was to consider the various precepts and edifications with a regular group of devotees who were seeking to better themselves regarding all things spiritual. There had also grown up a tendency, which some saw as a bit controversial, for a few to express their own imaginative experiences with voices and visions, and occasionally activities suggestive of psychic channeling.

The naive and altruistic young people who had gathered here, like many others, were assembled to become the flower of an era: a generation of peace, love, and understanding. All were expecting to become an integral part of the dawning of a new age of unprecedented spiritual enlightenment.

Guided by a small cadre of aging mentors, they would meet, discuss, share, and learn from one another while marveling at the teachings of both the ancient and the new that were being born into the tumultuous American culture during the late 1960s and early 1970s.

After some more chitchat and other pleasantries, Woody gathered up the assembled group of friends and acquaintances and ushered them downstairs where we were summarily stuffed into someone's aging station wagon. Then, with considerable blustering, frequent starts, stops, and lane shuffling, the driver dumped us out on a worn, cobbled sidewalk, next to a paint-spattered wall that was adorned with tattered posters.

I meandered through a long, dark alley with the other lemmings, eventually arriving at a newly discovered "underground restaurant." I think that meant that it had never seen a health inspector. It was so dark that reading the menu was barely an option. I finally gave up trying to follow the several dangling threads of frenzied conversation and politely choked down the supposedly authentic Middle Eastern cuisine.

Eventually, members of the group began a series of drawn out good-byes. As we retraced our steps, the troop began to disassemble in ones and twos, to catch cabs, buses or one of the underground trains that rumbled beneath our feet.

Woody and I returned to his apartment. I finally drifted off to sleep as he continued to reminisce about our college days in Old Main. When I awoke he was still talking.

The next day passed quickly. One of the groomsmen had made reservations for an impromptu bachelor party at the Playboy Club. We rather sheepishly ogled the scantily clad "bunnies," as the waitresses were called. I become almost incoherent after only one drink. Neither one of us was accustomed to the alcohol, but that didn't seem to curtail the rest of the party from enjoying themselves.

The next day we slowly meandered around the city while the reminiscing of college days began to take a more serious and markedly philosophical tone. It was the kind of reminiscing that is best left to the old and wise, reflecting back upon a long and productive life. Looking back, our conversation had that rather hollow and pretentious ring of young men who were just beginning their lives but acting as if they had suddenly become sages, merely because they were becoming cognizant of an impending rite of passage. We were rather abruptly realizing that we were being thrust into a new age of adult responsibilities. For better or for worse, richer or poorer, our youthful, relatively carefree college days were now forever behind us.

Claiming my privileges and responsibilities as best man, I finally asked Woody if he had forgotten that he had a wedding to attend and that perhaps we should return to the apartment, get changed, and get to the church. He drew a long, momentous breath, shuddered, and laughed. We hurried back from our legendary past, embraced our ominous present and prepared for an uncertain future.

As the wedding ceremony progressed, I felt like I had drifted into an altered state of consciousness. As the vows were exchanged, I found myself being absorbed into the mesmerizing eyes belonging to Susan, who just happened to be one of the bridesmaids. I knew exactly where she was even when I wasn't looking. When I did look, it was almost impossible to break my gaze. And she kept looking back, just as intently.

The rest of the assembled congregation seemed to fade and disappear. It felt as if we were transported to another time and place, a place so comfortable and familiar, yet not quite recognizable. I felt our souls once again acknowledge each other and begin to merge. We were both having the same experience.

I didn't understand it, nor did I question it; and neither did she. We just reveled in the midst of this divine witnessing.

Within this sacred knowing there was no need for the clutter of mindless words or the machinations of meaningless thought.

I found myself unable to respond to anyone but her. Without an utterance we both knew that our own betrothal and commitment had already been sealed—prophetically sealed, upon an altar of an ancient and sacred purpose. There was an acknowledgement and acceptance of an eternal reality, born ages ago before this present time had begun.

After the wedding she offered to show me her city. The ensuing day was a blur of museums and edifices. We visited the Empire State Building, and I think we took a ferry somewhere. It was as if we stood still and the world simply moved around us.

I remember walking very close and holding her hand as if it had always been there, waiting for me to claim it once more. Yet we never spoke of it. We simply knew and accepted. Reaching deeply into each soul's purpose, we also knew that the time was not yet right. But, we also knew the preparation would soon be complete.

Sergeant Hunter was graciously escorted to the airport and returned for duty in Fort Hood, Texas. The intensity and clarity born within New York City soon became some long ago dream that faded and then seemed to just drift away. It was back to the daily tasks of soldiering, or so I thought.

After a few months, I once again began to feel her presence. It kept increasing. It was everywhere, nourishing and comforting, but mostly just behind me and to my left. At one point, I completely expected to turn around and see her standing there; or at least to see her face behind me, in the scratched up mirror in the barrack's latrine where I conducted the daily ritual of shaving.

One day a bundle of her handwritten poetry arrived. The sensations and emotions were so strong that it was hard to focus on the words; words which wove a tapestry of feelings, thoughts, textures, and intensities. Her presence was somehow complete and resolute. Her soul continued to beckon to me from that ancient and still forgotten place.

It was the kind of presence that only on the rare occasion of a miracle is loaned by the creator to a favored Goddess. She was alive, right there beside me, before me, behind me, and within me. My heart was her heart. My breath was her breath. So I responded and called out to her, acknowledging her divinity.

My military leave opportunities had expired. I nervously croaked into the receiver of the pay phone, "Could you come visit me sometime?"

In a rather matter of fact manner she responded, "Yes."

I continued, "Can you come now?"

She hesitated for a moment then replied, "Of course. But, I can't be there until around noon tomorrow. The airlines said that would be the earliest I could get connections."

It was quite obvious that she had already inquired about travel arrangements. I was relieved and a little amused, but somehow not surprised.

Her flight was on one of those little commuter planes. She was the first passenger to appear through the small oval-shaped door. Retrieving two red canvas and leather bags, she strode across the tarmac like a fashion model. Her long hair gently bounced and fluttered as it embraced the prairie breeze that meandered across the airstrip. The sun was at her back, which left a slight impression of an other-worldly halo around her head.

Walking right up to me, she dropped the bags and held out her arms. We hugged. It was the kind of hug that lingers because neither wants to be the first to let go. After that reaffirming moment, we erupted with pleasantries and small talk. Being somewhat quiet and intense, I was rather surprised that I could actually do such a thing.

A few days before, I had emptied most of my savings account and purchased a small mid-sized station wagon. Reservations had been made at the Cow Palace, which at the time was the best Hotel in Killeen, although that wasn't saying much. On Sundays, I would sometimes take the post bus into town and sit in the adjoining coffee shop usually reading a book, which oddly enough was sometimes a military field manual.

Looking back, I find myself very amused and wondering what on earth was wrong with me. Guess I took my soldiering seriously. Anyway, it was good to have time to myself and to enjoy a hearty breakfast that didn't require standing in a line.

We took a rambling ride through Fort Hood and the adjoining community that ended with dinner back at the Cow Palace. We talked late into the night about everything and nothing. It was just good to be together. I had not presumed that we would be spending the night together; had really not thought that far ahead. Somewhere in the early morning hours we both fell asleep.

The next day we took a drive to Austin. If memory serves me correctly, we even took in a war protest at the University of Texas. The protests never made much sense to me. They just seemed angry, whiney, and impotent.

There were endless hours of chattering with a smattering of long, quiet pauses. It became apparent that we had some decisions to make. So late in the night I whispered, "It looks like we should just get married."

Susan smiled and nodded. We weren't quite sure how to do it. We had a small smattering of a family in Arizona and others in New York. Neither of us had much money, about six hundred dollars between us. So Texas seemed as good a place as any.

After all the sightseeing, I was a little short of cash so Susan paid for her own marriage license and blood test. We sauntered into the Court House in Temple, Texas and found a Baptist judge willing to accommodate our request for the commencement of nuptials. I remember it as a sort of odd and surreal encounter.

The judge had a rustic but beautifully appointed office with a lot of personal artifacts reflecting a rich Western heritage. The decor seemed to have come from a previous generation. I remember aged, wooden paneling and a magnificently carved desk. I think it was made of dark oak that had grown darker through the years. It was set in the midst of hundreds of faded books lining three walls. There were black-and-white pictures of bunk houses, wagons, cowboys, and horses.

He invited a clerk to be our witness and offered up some words of wisdom and advice for a new couple. I was so enamored of my beloved that I don't think I heard a thing. He had intense, patient eyes with a weathered face that suggested he had spent a good part of his life under the sun. His countenance left us with the impression that he had endured much, but had found a great peace and reverence in his life with just a touch of mischievous magic thrown in for fun. He was obviously a pious man. If anyone was worthy of sitting in judgment, it seemed that he was.

He made us feel like the occasion was as special for him as it was for us. Our vows were traditional; you know, "...for richer or for poorer, in sickness and in health, 'till death do us part ... ."

When asked, "Do you take this woman to be your lawfully wedded wife?"

I found myself saying, "Yes," to which this preacher-judge responded, "Well do you?" He inquired three more times. The words "I do" seemed to totally escape me. I looked blankly into his inquiring face without a clue as to why he kept asking, over and over again.

After enduring three courses of "yessing," he paused, turned to his assistant and murmured, "Well, I guess he does."

He held an exquisitely worn, itinerate preacher's manual and prayer book, which contained a faded purple ribbon attached to the binding. I could see notes in the margins and crumpled scraps of paper stuck between the pages. I wondered how many young soldiers he had introduced to the way of the householder during his ministry.

Upon conclusion of the ceremony, he smartly closed the sacred little book and gently set it on his desk. He clasped both our hands in his, and looked back and forth between us, looking deeply into of our eyes. He prayed over us, offering a blessing for what he called "... the beginning of your great adventure together."

Then, clearly I remember him saying, "Son, I have presided over many marriages and I want you to know that when she made her vows she meant it. I have no doubt that this is a marriage that will last, until death do you part."

He congratulated us and said something like, "Now go and love one another." He turned, slid his arms into a black pleated robe and disappeared out the door and down the corridor to his courtroom, his clerk shuffling behind with a cache of papers clenched in her arms.

We returned to Killeen and ate at the local Dairy Queen. Arriving at the airport just in time, I watched my newly sanctified wife disappear into a plane, which slowly ascended into the heavens from which she had come.

The next morning I awoke back at the barracks, listening to the distant prattle of a bugle playing revelry. Everything felt so odd, so out of place. Was it all a dream? Was it real? It all felt so right, but had happened so quickly. I was now a married man, but where was my wife? Where were the penetrating brown eyes belonging to my Lady Susan?

Pulling on my Cochran jump boots I exclaimed out loud "She's trapped in Babylon!"

It slowly dawned on me that I hadn't even notified my commanding officer, let alone requested permission for our nuptials. My primary post was to Company C, the Second Battalion of the Seventh Cavalry Regiment of the First Cavalry Division. However, I had been temporarily assigned to Darnell Army Hospital while being loaned to Command Programs, a new organization for a collection of services including race relations classes and a comprehensive substance abuse program. Of course, I was always available for "other duties as assigned."

Fortunately, at the time no one really knew who I was actually working for, as each organization tended to assume I belonged to the other. Meanwhile, my chain of command was a retiring Sergeant Major, a very "retiring" Lieutenant Colonel, and the Command Sergeant Major of the post; as well as a special task force Major, and of course, the Commanding General of the III Corps.

But, all of that is yet another story; just one more little story of the many stories—all woven together into the tapestry of the one big story that evolves into the magic that is our human experience.

Susan returned to New York where her friends had organized an impromptu wedding reception at the center. Three weeks later, I picked her up in a large rented station wagon that was offered as a wedding present by her mother. It was crammed full of all of Susan's earthly possessions. Within the month she found herself living in a trailer park in central Texas, a few miles from Fort Hood, married to an air-cavalry sergeant in the United States Army.

We had some built-in drawers and shelving in a closet, a bed, a table with two chairs, and a television offered as a wedding gift by my parents. There was also a sofa with a matching chair. Somewhere under all the padding, the frame for the sofa was broken and sagged so badly that it became the source of much amusement.

We truly didn't care. We mostly sat on the floor, looking at books and listening to the record player that was perched on a small bookcase we had made from four planks and a few cinder blocks. With my sergeant's pay and the marriage allotment that totaled almost six hundred dollars a month we were rich beyond our wildest dreams.

It was an exciting, magical time; a time in which anything was possible. We were young and infallibly committed. Our whole lives were before us. We were prepared and resolute; ready to do God's bidding to the best of our ability and understanding; eager to learn, to grow, perhaps to teach all that spirit was beginning to impart to us; and all for our own edification as well as for others.

We were here, at this perfect time and place; poised upon the brink of discovery as this new and golden age of Aquarius was being called forth.

I finally had to admit that, just maybe, something good could come out of New York City.

Chapter 3

Chosen

B y the end of the year, we were discharged from the army and headed toward Flagstaff for some graduate study at Northern Arizona University. Susan had been as far south as Guatemala and as far east as Austria, but had never been west of the Mississippi. For her, this would be a wild-west adventure. She had spent most of her life inside huge buildings, surrounded by concrete, asphalt, noisy traffic, and subways.

With the help of the G.I. bill, I was hoping to acquire a graduate degree in guidance and counseling. Fortunately, the army had already transported our hastily acquired twelve-by-sixty-foot Oakmont from Texas to a mobile home park at 398 Lake Mary Road. Dad had explained that trailer spaces were fairly hard to come by. But, he reasoned, we should be pleased with what he had found.

At my homecoming I was handed the spare key to the trailer along with a smashed packet, full of stained receipts and other documents that the driver left behind. I still recall the way that Dad licked his thumb, then separated and meticulously counted and planted several, crisp fifty-dollar bills in my hand, one at a time.

He seemed quite proud of being able to help us. My parents had decided that an additional wedding gift was to be funds for the installation of skirting around the bottom of the trailer. Fortunately, there would be enough cash left over for a small, but truly appreciated aluminum storage shed.

Our American Motors Sportabout was laboring up the road fully loaded with the bulk of our remaining personal belongings. We had just celebrated Christmas with my parents, near Phoenix, where I had retrieved belongings that had been stored when I enlisted. If memory serves me right, this was also the time that I lashed a small writing desk to the roof of the car, wrapped in an old military blanket. Plodding up the road with a homemade utility trailer listing to one side, and with the monotonous flapping of tattered blankets and tarps, we must have been quite a sight.

We had pulled off the road and onto crunching gravel in quest of a late breakfast at the only café in Cortes Junction. As Susan dashed out of the aging diner, she pulled the fur collar of her stylish jacket tightly around her ears. Then, with clenched hands plunged deep in her pockets she ran shivering back to the car, and immediately began pleading with the rather reluctant heater. It never did work right.

As we continued up the highway she became quiet, starring out the window toward the right side of the road; her long, cascading hair hid her expressive face from my view. I surmised that she was probably becoming a bit apprehensive about where we were going to live, and was most likely reflecting on how her life had been so abruptly transformed. I was taking her away from "The City," the only home she had ever known, away from her family, cherished friends, professional opportunities, and many treasured memories.

This was a cultured and sophisticated young woman who participated in costume designing for Broadway productions. She had started her own home-based clothing company and was selling some simple fashion accessories to high-end department stores. Designers were so intrigued with her ideas that some continued to seek her out, begging for sketches. I began to wonder; "My God, what was I thinking, taking this enchanting and talented woman from her home and budding career and dragging her off to such a remote and desolate place?"

It was not quite midmorning. In the dips and low areas, there were still episodes of hazy-gray fog, lazily drifting across the road. As we continued along in silence, the plethora of dark evergreens began crowding the edges of the highway, blocking the view of anything but the endless monotony of a giant frozen thicket.

The trees seemed to be in mournful agony, silently enduring the strain of the heavy weight of coagulated snow smashing and pulling at bowed and splintered branches. Occasionally, you would see the shuddering of a collapsing branch, or the gasp of a tortured tree, attempting to shake itself free of the hoary masses of frozen viscous that clung to every exposed inch of a bleak and oppressing landscape.

As we gained in elevation, the highway had become a sea of melting brown and yellow slush, spattering and spitting at the tires and windshields of all those who dared to traverse the slimy mucous. Here and there, mostly hidden in shade, the road would retract and form an unassuming glaze in an attempt to lure distracted or unsuspecting travelers. With one slight miscalculation you could be summarily dispatched from this intermittent skating rink and be helplessly hurled into an unforgiving ditch or craggy canyon.

As we rounded a treacherous curve, the piercing light of a nuclear sun maliciously bored into my painfully constricted eyes. This left me almost blind while hopelessly searching for a hint of the outline of the embattled causeway, fraught with danger and foreboding.

In the distance a cold and desolate mass of hoar-stained granite leered though the bent and tortured forest. These were touted as the great San Francisco Peaks, the highest point in all of Arizona and sacred to the Indians.

But all I could see out of the corner of my eye was my beloved's incredulity at all these sights, as she bowed her head for a moment and began to slowly move it from side to side in disbelief. Is this to be the place that she would have to endure in order to be with her woefully misguided husband?

As we approached the outskirts of the fledgling college town, we scrutinized scores of haphazardly parked eighteen-wheelers that had been helplessly stranded through the night, waiting for the melting of the polished sheets of black ice that clung relentlessly to the half-exposed highway. The trucks were spattered and dripping with the same festering ooze that we had encountered farther down the plateau.

Occasionally, a driver would emerge from an encrusted cab, jump down into the quagmire and scurry back and forth checking chains, tires, and cargo before returning to the warm sanctuary where acrid plumes of diesel fumes kept both weary men and droning engines warm and alive.

Covering the entire town was a putrid low-lying, brownish-yellow scum that was belching forth from a thousand fireplaces and woodstoves, where families huddled together hoping to stave off the freezing cold. The choking smoke irritated my nose and throat and made my eyes start to tear.

Apparently, the full impact of this visage was so disturbing that my newly begotten bride opted to remain silent as we reluctantly approached what was to be our new home.

Just south of town, heading out toward the west, we cautiously traversed Lake Mary Road. After driving a few hundred yards we discovered Aspen Village trailer park. It was wedged between bowed trees succumbing to the cruel winter onslaught. Sloshing through a few hundred feet of melting mud and snow, we found our Oakmont; filthy, spattered with dirt, wheels partially removed, and not anywhere near level. I thought that perhaps I should consider a motel room while we got things sorted out, but that would be much too expensive with our meager funds. Besides, classes at NAU would be starting in less than a week.

I felt so defeated. My head bowed, I was unable to make eye contact with my beloved. My heart felt like a collapsed lung. Working up a little courage, I forced myself to turn to her. She looked at me with great emotion, trembling, with tears in her eyes. Her lips began so quiver and then she sobbed.

"My God, this place is so beautiful! I had no idea that you were bringing me to a place that would be so spectacular and magical!"

Apparently, she was under the impression that we were going to a landscape that looked like the lifeless deserts in the old black-and-white, John Wayne movies. She had not expected to see forests, mountains or lakes in Arizona. We held each other for the longest time, then returned to the car and unhooked the utility trailer. It was obvious that I had a lot to learn about this marvelous creature. Fortunately, I would have a lifetime.

The Dairy Queen was closed, so we decided to celebrate with lunch at the Taco Bell, located just outside of the south entrance to the university. It was a joyous feast.

We rejoiced in our good fortune. Our little home would be nestled within an enchanted forest, graced by the purity of newly fallen snow adorning rich, evergreen branches. The sky once again opened into a vibrant royal blue, and the sun seemed to blaze forth with great warmth and approval. The peaks, guardians of the way, stood proud, majestic, and serene; while intermittent, playful little breezes enticed frozen crystals that danced playfully around our footsteps.

You see, it's all in your perspective!

As we returned to our Oakmont, we found a fast moving crew shouting and industriously pumping jack handles, while rearranging gray cement blocks and wooden shims beneath our modest mobile home. A stout, boistress gentlemen strode over to me, looked me in the eye and sounded off with "Welcome home boy!" He ripped off a glove and grabbed my hand and almost took off my arm. He was a veteran from a previous war.

He immediately took charge, quickly explaining that he would make sure that water, natural gas, and electricity would all be safely hooked up before sundown. He cautioned me that I should get an electrical heat tape around the water line as soon as possible, before it froze. He even suggested where I could get one. All the utilities would be included in the lease except for electricity. He also explained that in the spring we would best have the trailer re-leveled, as it would most likely settle when the ground thawed out for summer.

This was the park manager. It turned out that he and my dad spent some time over a couple of beers getting to know each other. His son had also enlisted, but he didn't make it back home. Hearing that I was coming home from the Army with a new bride, and going back to school, he decided to take us under his wing. He even helped me get some part-time construction work.

And thus began the next phase of our adventure together. Susan embraced her new life and never looked back, denying that she ever missed the city and the creative career opportunities that had once captured so much of her energy and attention.

The time in Flagstaff passed quickly. Along the way Susan's mother moved in with us. By age and disposition she was no longer able to survive on her own. We were also blessed by the birth of our first child, via the Lamaze natural childbirth method. She was a very noisy and energetic young lass who delighted in singing to the sun each morning.

Upon graduation we moved to Tucson where my newly acquired degree brought improved employment opportunities. Susan was very happy to quit her part-time job as a collection agent in a credit company. She had considered becoming a chiropractor, but made the decision to become a mother and homemaker instead. One day, agreeing to do some emergency typing for a friend, she discovered the freelance court reporting and transcribing business. Her skills were such that she was soon juggling several clients. As computer hardware and software advanced, she was on the leading edge of the implementation of several computer-assisted court transcription systems.

Before the advent of this technology, most court reporters would sit near the front of the courtroom utilizing a machine called a stenograph. It produced a series of cryptic abbreviations that were printed on an almost endless roll of stacked, adding-machine-sized paper. The court stenographer would thus record the proceedings by means of a shorthand language that was imprinted by stroking a keyboard that involved depressing several keys at once to produce the inked imprints.

The language used by these methods was more akin to how words sound rather than how they are actually spelled. In order to keep up with the normal pace of human speech, there were a multitude of abbreviations that provided for many commonly used and some not-so-commonly used phrases. Later, outside of the courtroom or deposition site, this specialized encrypted language had to be translated and transcribed.

At the conclusion of proceedings, most court reporters would return to their offices or work at home late into the night—translating and reading out loud into a tape recorder, speaking precisely (complete with punctuation), the exact instructions, testimonies, arguments and rulings as they were conducted during the court's proceedings.

Then, transcribers would listen to the taped recordings and carefully render a typewritten transcript, which the court reporter would then review, correct, and certify as being accurate. Sometimes court reporters would do their own typing, but most utilized the services of someone like Susan.

With the advance of computer technology, a magnetic cassette tape could record the encrypted strokes on the improved and enhanced stenograph. Later, the cassette could be placed in a computer that would record and translate both the notes and a rough draft of a readable transcript. However, the finalized version still required competent operators to precisely edit the transcript, via the personal computer, in order to render an accurate and professional product that would still have to be laboriously printed and collated.

These new systems allowed the transcriber to read the encrypted notes while at the same time editing the rough draft translation that showed up on the monitor. Meanwhile, there was still a hard copy of the inked notes in the paper tray, located below the stenograph, that could be stored and utilized in the event of some electronic malfunction.

This whole process almost tripled the amount of time that a court reporter could be available to take depositions, thereby greatly increasing the number of transcripts that a court reporter could produce. There was no longer a need to sit for hours dictating into a microphone, making an audio tape to be played back later so it could be typed.

Now, a rough draft could be sent by modem to a competent transcriber, with encrypted note-reading skills, who in turn, could render the finished product in a fraction of the time that straight typing would require. Since the transcripts are paid for by the page, this was a great boon to the profession.

And, it was perfect for Susan. She could stay home in her office; be available whenever the children needed her, and work around their schedules as well as her own. Her skills were exquisite, so she could almost have her pick of the several court reporters clamoring to work with her. She often had a long waiting list.

Once two reporters actually engaged in a serious verbal altercation regarding whose work should have priority. Of course, the choice was Susan's, not theirs.

Some might see this as very tedious work, and for sure it was. But, it also offered a lifetime of intricate glimpses into all kinds of subjects. She knew a multitude of things about medical procedures and practices. She learned about water rights, mining and mineral exploration, corporate taxing strategies, how airplanes are built and maintained. She once even had a case about interstate rail transportation, and on and on ... .

She learned intimate details of political figures and, of course, became expert in how law is practiced. Thus, her "little business," as she called it, offered her a life of limitless information and stories on a wide variety of subjects and events.

We had become typical householders. Soon our second child was born. This young man came with an iron will. You could inspire him, but he was one who would not be ruled. We enjoyed our home immensely. We had a whole acre of natural Sonoran Desert, right next to the historic Old Spanish Trail. And, there was not an apartment building or subway in sight. Susan became quite fond of the desert, which she now celebrated as being full of life and magic.

Of course, we maintained our keen interest in things metaphysical, taking classes and establishing friendships with some of the folks at a local ashram. Susan even did some transcribing for a local psychic that some claimed rivaled Edgar Cayce's capacities and insights.

There was even time to participate in the building of a small youth camp down south in Arivaca, near the Mexican border, where I first discovered my interest in real estate investment. And, it was always a treat to head for the Catalina Mountains just north of the city for a leisurely picnic.

We dissected books, devoured movies, mused, meditated, loved, fought, and machinated about the issues of the day, both large and small. In short, we celebrated all the joys and travails of a modern American family.

In the spring of 1985, we were still making payments on the little travel trailer that was parked along the side of our ranch-style, slump-block home. Before we were able to get into the larger house, Susan had sometimes used it as an office where she could concentrate on her transcribing. I had even surprised her with the installation of a window-mounted air conditioner. During the hot summer nights we sometimes slept in the trailer, since the less efficient swamp cooler struggled just to keep the house a few degrees cooler during the monsoon season and subsequent increased humidity.

But now I had converted the little travel trailer into a cozy chapel. It was a bit too small to consider doing any serious yoga. However, it was an excellent place to conduct some quality reflection, prayer, and meditation. I had even crafted a special bookshelf that contained a selection of our favorite sacred texts. Susan had designed some curtains that really set the mood. And, with some candles and incense, it became the perfect little chapel. It was also a good place for a time out from the rigors of a young family with two small children and from what was becoming a rather antagonistic, in-residence mother-in-law.

At the time, I was beginning to experience an ever-increasing sense of communion with distant rivers, forests, valleys, and mountains. Sometimes, during early morning meditation, it was almost as if I would find myself transported; sitting on some knoll on the foothills near the mountains of my childhood home in Colorado.

Sitting in meditation, I could feel the cool breezes on my skin, hear the rattle of aspen leaves and see up into the high alpine basins. I once found myself standing atop a craggy outcropping of a high windswept promontory, gazing upon crystal clear waterfalls. Far below in the valley, I could make out Telluride, that haunted little mining town of my youth.

These experiences were becoming so real that at times I was startled to open my eyes and to realize that I was still sitting in the little trailer next to our slump-block house in the desert on the outskirts of Tucson. There was this tremendous drawing, a calling to go back to the mountains in Telluride. But, it made no sense to me. Our home, work, and family were all in southern Arizona. What sense would it make to uproot ourselves.

Yet the calling endured.

One spring day in March, everything began to change. It had been a long and stressful week. I was fond of rising early, taking a short jog along a desert path, and then sitting in meditation at the back of the house. Our home was on a modest ridge with the back of the house facing a gentle north-facing slope, looking up into the Catalina foothills. I remember taking extra time to enjoy all the special sights and sounds of the awakening spring desert. Yet, the ever-increasing restlessness, a sense of imminent change, kept pulling at my soul.

Meanwhile, Susan was at her wits' end. She had been working late into the night, trying to meet a deadline for a court case that was being appealed. Stepping back into the house, I again began to hear the rattling of her keyboard. It was said that she could type faster than a person could talk. Well, that was perhaps a bit of an exaggeration, but she was pretty fast.

Sensing my presence behind her, she stood up, moved around her ergonomically correct chair, gathered up her long hair, pulled it to one side, and plopped face down on the carpet; placing her hands above her head.

"Please." She instructed.

There was a rather cranky misalignment in her upper spine. Long hours of typing did not help the condition. On occasion, she would get so uncomfortable that muscle spasms could produce headaches that brought tears to her eyes. Her chiropractor had given us instructions on how to make a simple thoracic adjustment, which seemed to relieve her discomfort, at least temporarily.

I began gently massaging the offended area, and launched a couple of short, quick, downward pulses which yielded the appreciated "pop." She released a long blissful sigh, rested a moment, jumped up, and proclaimed.

"I'm going to need some help today. You'll have to get Ben ready. I think Jessica is ready to go."

As I stepped into the long hallway I encountered a gleeful five-year-old Benjamin charging down the hallway, half naked, and absconding with one of his sister's shoes. Nine-year-old shoeless Jessica was screeching after him in hot pursuit; with an out-of-breath and much annoyed mother-in-law lumbering after them.

Susan's mother, Mollie, had assembled something on the table that sort of resembled breakfast. Before long, we had things sorted out and I was trudging down the winding road with our progeny to the local bus stop.

It was a daily ritual in which I escorted Jessica to the corner in an effort to protect her from some older boys who were a bit rowdy. It took some doing, but eventually we were able to convince Jessica that if she didn't run from the boys, they couldn't chase her. I think she has been in charge ever since.

At the bus stop, I liked to sit cross-legged on a berm where we could wait for the bus. It was a joy to just watch the kids interact, learn, and grow. My bushy-blond beard and long ponytail made some of the neighborhood a bit uneasy. But, the "biker" inmates at the Pima County Jail where I worked didn't seem to mind; and, neither did the administration when they needed a corrections specialist who could quietly find out what was happening on the other side of the bars. But that is yet another story. There is always a multi-verse of little stories within the one big story.

Toddler Ben could never seem to understand why he couldn't go with Jessica on the bus. We had finally landed a slot in a nearby pre-school. Ben of course, was convinced that he was going to a real school and Jessica was just going to a pretend school.

After delivering Ben to his academy, I headed off to a day of professionalism at the local corrections facility. It all seemed like a normal day at the Hunter household, but providence had something else in mind for us.

When I arrived home that evening, Susan rushed to the door and immediately announced. "Well, I made it, and with time to spare!"

That really wasn't all that unusual, somehow she always managed to get her rush jobs done on time. Her reliability was just one of the things that made her such a valuable commodity.

Then she declared, "I think I have earned dinner and a movie. Mollie can take care of the kids. What do you think?"

I had no objections.

We probably ate at the Good Earth restaurant. I have no idea what may have been showing at the El Con theatre.

After the movie, we took the long way home. I remember the moon, shining brightly across the rolling Sonoran landscape with its abundance of palo verde, mesquite, creosote, and cactus.

As I turned off the headlights, the tires crunched up the hill through the oversized gravel that lined our driveway. We were not blessed with streetlights, so all that the heavens had to offer could be seen and enjoyed. We sat in our little blue Fiat, talking and cherishing the moment.

As our eyes adjusted to heaven's glow, we lingered, sitting back in our seats with open windows, enjoying the cool evening air, wistfully focused on a cloudless, star-filled sky. Life was good.

Then everything became intensely still and silent. My entire body began to tingle, as if it had been asleep, but was now awakening. Waves of shimmering energy began to surround us. We seemed to be caught within a glowing veil of translucent light. With eyes wide open, I turned to my beloved who appeared as a radiant, shimmering column of energy. Rather laboriously, then clearly, I began to hear an unfamiliar voice drone on from out of her mouth.

I heard the words "When the earth comes 'round twice; His torch shall blaze in the skies."

We sat motionless for a time. The energy began to subside. Slowly we recovered our earthly faculties. We were awestruck. There had been an opening. Susan was trance channeling. Some unknown source was manifesting through her. And, there was a message. We were excited. We were full of apprehension and questions.

We went into the house. Susan sat down and the voice continued. I grabbed a tape recorder and fumbled with the buttons and dials as the words resumed. Some general greetings and explanations were offered.

This "Source," as it described itself, "was coming to comfort and to guide through a difficult but fruitful transition." We were told that there would be instructions offered to make the opening of the channel easier and more complete. We prayed, and sat in meditation for awhile, asking for guidance and protection for whatever righteous purpose that there may be. ...

Then we were told, "Go to the mountain."

A few moments later it was suggested that we go outside and look up into the heavens. From out of a cloudless sky we watched a huge circular formation of billowing white clouds appear right above us, several thousand feet over our neighborhood. Then it turned into one huge dome-shaped disc and dissipated as quickly as it had formed, leaving the sky clear once more.

There was the admonition, "Lest ye doubt."

The scriptures say that many are called, but few are chosen. Clearly, this one had been chosen. Thus began the next phase of our adventure.

Chapter 4

The Adventure Continues

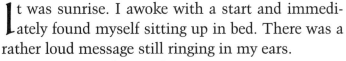

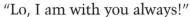

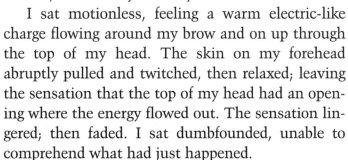

I t was sunrise. I awoke with a start and immediately found myself sitting up in bed. There was a rather loud message still ringing in my ears.

"Lo, I am with you always!"

I sat motionless, feeling a warm electric-like charge flowing around my brow and on up through the top of my head. The skin on my forehead abruptly pulled and twitched, then relaxed; leaving the sensation that the top of my head had an opening where the energy flowed out. The sensation lingered; then faded. I sat dumbfounded, unable to comprehend what had just happened.

Susan rolled over, looked at me for a moment, and sat up slowly, inquiring in a rather matter-of-fact manner:

"Lo, I am with you always?"

Our heads nodded in unison. She had heard the same thing at the same time, but seemingly without a "dumbfounded" response.

This "Source" explained that we were a bifurcated channel that would serve as one. This allegedly obvious condition was one that I was never able to adequately comprehend or accept. We were supposedly like two poles of one energy—male and female. Susan was dubbed "the channel that speaks" and I was dubbed "the channel that does not speak."

Supposedly our initial coming together served as an incubation period that eventually allowed the Source to come forth. It was explained that if we had not come together, the Source would not have been able to manifest.

We were instructed to meditate together on a daily basis. In the evenings, we were to be given further instructions and explanations. A diet was recommended "in order to strengthen and purify the physical bodies." It was a basic rotation diet which included three days of fruit with yogurt or cottage cheese followed by three days of rice with steamed vegetables—two from above the ground; one from below. Then, three days of fresh green salads with small amounts of broiled fish or poultry.

There was also the constant reminder, "Drink! Drink! Drink!" Preferably, a "good quality" water. The diet seemed harmless enough and fairly healthy so we gave it a try.

The first few sessions were a bit ominous and intense to say the least. We sat on the floor in the privacy of our bedroom on white sheepskins and old military blankets. Sometimes there would be contact and the Source would come through, and sometimes it would not. Susan would usually sit cross-legged in a meditative position and offer a prayer before we would begin. She would clasp her hands together and hold them at the center of her chest.

Sometimes she would start to tremble and shake and softly moan. It looked like she was hanging on for dear life. This shaking occurred only five or six times. Once, the shaking became quite dramatic; I wondered if she were going to start bouncing off the floor. Susan's body temperature would rise dramatically; her eyes would tear and her nose would run. She would sweat like a woman in labor.

The Source explained that this was all a part of "... the process of the rising of the energies and the purification of the channel." We were both directed to take certain vitamins and minerals. Though it didn't make much sense to me, we were told to basically eat the same things because it would tend to "harmonize the energies within the bodies and make the opening easier."

Susan engaged in a sort of ritual bathing, which was concluded with the gentle massaging of certain oils into various areas of her body that the Source referred to as "moon centers." One evening, during meditation, she abruptly came to her feet, looking as if she were a puppet that had been pulled up by a string attached to the top of her head.

Moving like an automaton, she went to the shower and let the water run hot. Her head twisted and contorted at angles that I did not think were possible. A loud cracking and popping erupted from the base of her skull and neck.

Susan seemed to resurface as she let out her typical long, blissful sigh, and abruptly exclaimed, "My God, how did that happen?"

The Source later explained that the adjustment was necessary for the proper alignment for channeling, and that now the initial transition was complete. Throughout all the succeeding years, this shaking and discomfort was never witnessed again.

When the Source would begin to "come through," as we called it, Susan's voice would change. Often it took on a deep, powerful, and authoritative tone that inspired a sense of compliance and loyalty. At other times, her pitch would be much higher; with a sort of gentle, sublime nature reflecting a sense of serenity and bliss. The speech had a sort of measured cadence that was radically unlike her normal pattern of speech.

In addition to the tone and phrasing of speech, the choice of words and verbal expressions used were somewhat alien to her usual presentation. In short, few if any of the channel's individual characteristics and personality were present. Anyone in attendance could tell that something very unusual was happening.

Susan, the channel, would comment that she was mostly oblivious to what was transpiring. She would sometimes report that she could hear a faint voice talking as if at a great distance, but she was unable to understand what it was saying. At other times she was aware that her mouth, tongue, and lips were moving, and were somehow out of her control.

On occasion, she said she could "listen in" but had a problem with anticipating what was going to be said. So, her voice would begin to pause, stutter or misspeak. The channel who does not speak noticed that, at these times, the channeling would be suspended for a moment, as if the Source was recalibrating or rebooting. Then, the channeling would begin again.

The speaking channel once remarked that something completely "took her out." We were later told that this action had been taken because she was getting so interested and enthralled about what was being said that she was interrupting and making it difficult to complete the reading.

Upon conclusion of a session, Susan would take a few deep breaths, sometimes sigh or perhaps release a short, soulful whimper. Then, she would open her eyes and look around the room for a moment, as if she were trying to figure out where she was. We would then discuss in general terms what had been received from the Source.

As I would speak, she would often begin to remember and start repeating some of the words, verbatim. She said it was like waking up and remembering parts of a dream. The speaking channel avoided listening to any of the tapes for fear of what she called "contamination." She decided early on that this Source would let her know if she ever needed to know anything. The Source concurred. And it did give her further information; rather incessantly at times.

In the beginning Susan said she experienced a tremendous amount of energy. Although we never experienced any blinking lights or bouncing furniture, the channeling did seem to take its toll on her. The Source likened the phenomenon to an incandescent lightbulb. As the energies began to flow throw her, the resistance, as it was called, tended to hold on, or to clutch right down into the cellular level, thus creating fatigue.

At other times, the forces that were working through her seemed to be able to redirect this energy, thus creating a healing effect. This was seen as part of her karmic burden as a channel, for she had brought forth this gift before, so we were told, "in many times, in many ways, in many places."

As the channel's capacity expanded, it became more and more unnecessary to go into an obvious, and deep, trance state in order to make contact. As the process continued, step by step, she was able to hear and meld with the energies that would bring so much information, both mundane and profound.

The goal was to become "a working partner in the daily lives of the entities." She eventually was able to bring the Source's messages from a conscious state while conducting all the tasks of a normal householder.

During these initial sessions, she reported having visions of ancient symbols, sometimes coming together to form a sort of emblematic shield. Some were recognized as Atlantian or Lemurian in origin. Some were more universal. During one session, there seemed to be a bit of consternation because I was not able see these images; images that were supposedly forming right before me. I began to quietly wonder if the channel that "does not speak" was also one that "does not see."

I tended to chase Susan around with a portable tape recorder in an effort to capture every potentially channeled word. It was decided that this was "a good and useful effort." However, at other times I was admonished to just relax and allow myself to become part of the process that was unfolding "without the distraction of tending to the recording devices."

As the channel opened and cleared, we were instructed to have each member of the household be presented with an opportunity for a personal reading. There was special interest in addressing the children and their questions so that they might better understand what was going on with Mom. Of course, Dad had a few questions too!

Mollie, Susan's mother, seemed accepting; but basically found the whole thing to be a bit amusing. The kids tended to take it all in stride, perhaps being too young to fully realize just how out of the ordinary the situation was becoming.

We were told that, within this time and culture, there had been the beginning of an awakening and remembering of the spiritual nature of man. And of course, that also included womb-men.

It was explained that this was "all part of an initial transitional phase of gifted psychics, channels, and seers that were ushering a new way of thinking and understanding into the popular public domain, and thus into the forefront of the modern culture."

The purpose of all this skullduggery was to offer a catalyst to inspire the imagination and awaken the mind of an emerging generation.

The Source further explained that this current manifestation of the God Head (Susan's Source) would be "less concerned with the wonderings and musings of curious minds and more involved with the direction and reunification of evolving souls, seeking manifestation of the divine nature within the earthly realms."

We were told that this "Source" would always tell the truth, but it may not always be what people wanted to hear.

Before long it was announced that there was to be the presentation of a series of readings for public distribution; but now and then, as time allowed, there would also be opportunity for personal readings. It was explained that "the essential message and work of this particular manifestation of the Source was not so much for the masses as it is for the edification and fulfillment of ancient promises that were made to the few who may now respond to this particular material through these particular channels."

So I immediately sprang into action, purchased some state-of-the-art recording equipment and authored a simple brochure outlining a process for folks to come and discover what was going on in the master bedroom in a little house on the desert just outside of Tucson.

First, the Source provided a series of readings, which were simply entitled, "Readings on the Resurrection." Next came, "Readings on the Feminine Nature." Eventually there would be other collections of readings.

We made written transcripts of the proceedings along with cassette-tape copies of these sessions for anyone who might be interested. As the time of this publication transcripts of the readings are still available, free of charge, on the Internet at **www.readingsfromthesource.com**.

Our activities were dubbed, "Readings to the Children of the Light." Guided by the Source, a logo was created representing the spirit of the work at hand. It came from one of the visions offered to Susan at the time of her opening as "the channel who speaks."

Surprisingly (it was then; but not so surprising now) most of our friends didn't seem to think much of the events we were describing. There was an understandable tendency to coyly withhold judgment while not really expressing much follow-up interest. But there were a select few who immediately embraced all that the readings had to offer.

We even tried a few expensive, but well-placed, ads to see what response there might be. The Source seemed to take a sort of philosophical tone; suggesting that although not financially fruitful, the people who needed exposure to the information had been drawn to the logo and had in fact responded.

Nevertheless, before long, mainly due to word of mouth, a trickle of requests for personal readings began. The Source suggested that before receiving a personal reading, applicants should become familiar with the "series readings," as we called them, so that there would be some understanding of the nature and purpose of the Source as manifested through this particular channel.

This was not to be a Source that would expend the channel's energies offering hundreds or thousands of personal readings for a fee. It would not make itself available at our whim, but rather when it surmised that the "purposes were correct and the time was right." Questions would not be answered simply because they were asked. This Source would sometimes withdraw for days or weeks at a time, while we wondered when or if it would return.

Eventually, this Source became an integral part of our life, at times offering almost constant insights, explanations, and observations along with the occasional recommendations. These were supposedly required to avoid some of the major pitfalls that we might have experienced upon this path, of totally unanticipated events, that were soon to "come burgeoning forth upon us."

It was explained that this arrangement was agreed upon long before we made the commitment to come into this particular incarnation.

The Source was always respectful of our personal opinions, daily duties, and mundane schedules. It was generally quick to point out that what was offered were always to be seen as recommendations; and, it was ever by choice, day by day, that one's path is trod.

But, it was hard not to follow these "recommendations," sometimes rather blindly—especially when directions seemed urgent, and there was apparently not always time to explain, or ability to comprehend why the direction was necessary and what possible unpleasant consequences might result if this benevolent guidance were ignored.

In all, only a few dozen people received personal readings. However, the evolving connection and communication with family members and close friends would eventually become prolific, covering almost every subject imaginable. Meanwhile, it became abundantly clear that most people were more interested in simply knowing a psychic channel than in showing any interest in responding to the advice and opportunities that was being offered through the Source's discourses.

Before long, the Source would only become available to a few, who occasionally came across our path. Again, it was explained that the intent was to teach us how to become "conscious beings that did not have to go into a trance or go to sleep to communicate with the creator."

It reminded us that this Source had manifested for other reasons than to be a teacher for the masses; it was destined to become more of a personal experience which one day should be written about. And that, in time, this would all become clear to the entities involved.

There was a consistent theme: We were not just living on the brink of a so called "new age," but rather as a culmination of several previous ages. We were supposedly entering a period that will either be a challenging but predominantly gentle evolution, or a disastrous plunge into a painful crucifixion. Much of what was offered was similar to and a confirmation of information that had come from other contemporary sources and psychics, but our "window" seemed to have a few unique twists.

At times, there was an almost desperate plea to embrace the sacred ways before a potential for world calamity would become almost inevitable. It was explained over and over how we were on the cusp of massive political and social change. It would supposedly come at a speed and with an intensity that heretofore would be almost unimaginable. Much of it would have to do with a geometrical progression in technology that was as yet still in its infancy.

Popular prophecies were confirmed and expanded upon regarding increase propensity toward devastating earthquakes in the West Coast of America, the Great Northwest, the Great Lakes area, and New York City. It was suggested that we should expect catastrophic geological upheavals on an unprecedented scale that would become increasingly destructive over the decades to come.

There was discussion of the possibility of losing one- to two-thirds of the planet's population due to war, disease, and famine. There were also explanations of growing astronomical influences that could result in polar shifting.

In addition to the reshaping of the American continent, the submerging of parts of Europe, Japan, and India were discussed. However, always we were cautioned that this would not be as one massive cataclysmic event, but rather a slowly moving but ever-quickening process that could take several generations.

There was criticism of how some scientists were experimenting with biochemical and ion-based research that could become exceedingly destructive and have far-reaching impacts. It was explained that as yet there was not sufficient wisdom and maturity within the existing political matrix, which had no way of controlling or even understanding their mistakes in judgment until it might be too late.

In the arrogant quest for power and dominion could come the unbalancing of the natural ecosystem and prove to be the gravest error of all. It was suggested that there is more to fear from a new ice age than from global warming. Episodes of geologic and climatic change were seen as natural and cyclic—good for the overall health of the planet.

It was explained that the earth, as well as the other planets, has its own natural cycles. Although mankind could influence much, it was considered to be arrogance and folly to assume that humanity would ever have the capacity to destroy the world. Rather, it is a partnership between the different life forms to create the opportunities for each expression of life, in order to manifest and experience that which is its own inherent nature. No one life form ever has control over all the realms and ecologies of existence. It was described as more of an evolving collaborative process with mankind as the most recent and novel advancement.

When the balance is disturbed it will always right itself, but sometimes with catastrophic effects for those who are present in body during these rectifying processes. Again, the process may be slow and evolutionary or abrupt and destructive; but always the result is restoration of the balance. And, this was considered to be as true for humankind as for the planet as a whole, with its myriad of life forms both seen and unseen.

This Source often spoke like this, sounding vague and obscure to those of us who listened. Sometimes it was up to us to seek clarification; at other times, seeming to sense our confusion, a simpler more descriptive rendition would be tendered.

It was explained that this is not the most technologically advanced civilization that has ever been on earth. Civilizations much greater than this one have been obliterated from the planet. It is supposedly hard for us to recognize this because of the short-sighted perceptions we have regarding how long human beings have been on the earth.

It was explained that human history should not be measured in mere thousands of years; but rather hundreds of thousands of years. It was also explained that the nature and focus of souls that manifested in flesh bodies within the earth changed and evolved over time. Four major waves or "entries" of souls were described with a fifth one scheduled that had already begun to arrive.

The reality of the arrival of this new "partner" in our lives that simply called itself the "Source" was a bit perplexing. We thought we had graduated past the elementary stages of dabbling in channeling and psychics. We had decided that no matter how interesting or inspiring the information from a psychic might be, in the end, one has to be willing to stand on one's own insights and conclusions.

Ultimately, this is just another source of information. You will eventually make a decision; to embrace and to believe, or not to believe, or to simply pick and choose. But this wasn't merely some abstract fascination or mental machination that you can simply entertain or dismiss.

Now, we were in the midst of it. It had become part of us, and we a part of it. What might other people think of a family that had such strange goings-on? What would be the effect on friendships and the children?

It had been awhile since the Source had presented itself to the channel. Then, one evening, after the children were asleep, while we pondered these things, the Source once again responded.

"SOURCE: We would seek this night to respond to that which is the inquiry of these who are serving as the vessels of the light - - must understand and accept that which is to be as known to the conscious mind as the opening of the door, as the accepting of the burden of the mission, is to be accomplished, as has been given.

So are those many hundreds as the entity to whom we speak, have they been touched, have some responded, have some as been as reluctant in the process of opening and surrendering.

So, as the necklace is strung with the pearls of the reflected and resurrected light, grown into full glory by the friction of the testing in the fire of the experience of each individual, so is the strength of the strand made as invincible.

Such are the interruptions, as the entities see them, in the onslaught of readings as they began. So was the foundation forged, so was the way made open.

That for the present is the attention of these eternal forces focused upon others at the moment, to strengthen - - that the entities may - - to have this time, this lull in the storm, as it were, to strengthen that which is the discipline, to harmonize self in consciousness with that which has been given as the guidelines upon which the lifestyle may be based.

That those ties which bind the entities to that which is the life circumstances in this area [Tucson] before the transition is made to that which is the meridian point - - so must this all be gathered up as within a package to be stored, to be put aside, that the future may begin in earnest, unencumbered, untethered; that the full blossoming may continue, may reach its fullest potentiality.

That this is the time, that this is the energy that is being developed that is and must always be seen by the entities as a conscious, cooperative - - yea, a conversation, as it were, between levels of existence, as the attuning into the infinite becomes more natural and more readily accessible to the entities.

Such are the guideposts given along the way. Such is the contact that we maintain with thee daily, constantly, but that it takes as a different form at this time. Lest the entities become as disturbed, as the need is great, so shall we manifest in this way.

Know and believe that the promises as given are real; that this is, may we repeat, a lifetime process, and to remind the entities that as the transition and the foundations are finally laid in the area of that which is Ajax [a mountain in Colorado], so will the merging with this divine energy become as a continuous and constant force, as a continuous and constant experience; that at that time will the visitations, as it were, the readings, as they are called, become as a constant and ongoing thing."

So we yielded to the intense calling of the mountain, and the words of this "Source." Remembering the admonition of "Go to the mountain," we responded and made our commitment to wholeheartedly embrace the emerging adventure.

We were bound to Telluride: the sacred valley ... .

Chapter 5

Telluride:
The Sacred Valley

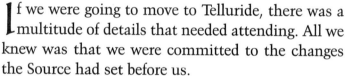

I f we were going to move to Telluride, there was a multitude of details that needed attending. All we knew was that we were committed to the changes the Source had set before us.

The equity from the three rentals would come in handy if we were to successfully relocate to Colorado. Reluctantly, I sold my motorcycle and the little travel trailer that we had converted to a meditation chapel. We didn't know how it would all work out. We just knew that the Source was with us and we were on our way to the Sacred Valley.

We also needed to dispose of a remaining ten acres located about an hour south of Tucson in a place along the Mexican border called Arivaca. The area had been ranch land, which had been received in a territorial land grant that extended clear back to the Gadsden Purchase.

We had stretched ourselves in order to purchase twenty acres with owner financing. It turned out to be a good investment. After paying off the well, I divided the acreage into two, ten-acre parcels; selling one ten-acre parcel for what I had originally paid for the entire twenty. So, essentially we got ten acres for free, except for some sweat equity and other miscellaneous improvements.

The rolling terrain was adorned with a rambling, hunter-green forest of sweet-smelling mesquite trees. It was interspersed with little grassy meadows that had faithfully fed wandering cattle through the generations.

A local cat skinner helped me put in a stock pond at the bottom of a narrow intermittent wash. It was complete with a well-engineered spillway and an extensive, hand-laid riprap lining of country rock. At the time we thought it was quite an impressive achievement. We were proud of it.

In the monsoon season you could hear a motley chorus of frogs blissfully crooning in the moonlight. During the dry, parched months the wind would sometimes caress miniature sand dunes of loose rippling earth that danced around the once lush clumps of green grasses that had become brown and brittle.

Around the perimeter of the property I had erected a four-strand, barbed-wire fence. It took awhile to complete, as I had to work on it intermittently, a little at a time, during weekends.

The well had come in around 60 feet. With an eight-inch casing, it produced all the water that we could pump. We talked of using the property as some kind of family retreat in a vague and distant future. Actually, we didn't really know what we were going to do with it. It just seemed like something good to do. One summer we even let some folks graze a few cattle on it.

It was simply a cherished little place to spend an occasional weekend. It was a welcomed contrast from the stark, concrete corrections environment where I had been employed. It was good to feel the wind in your hair, the sun on your shoulders, and the earth beneath your feet.

It just felt good to get out of town and enjoy "being on the land" as Suzy called it. Looking back, I think it was a place to simply brush off the regimentation of civilization, take a deep re-laxing breath, and dream our dreams.

Just down the road from our acreage, Mark and Wendy were seeking to establish a back-to-the-earth, sixties lifestyle. They lived simply out of an aging mobile home with an extra room added to one side. At the time, Mark took odd jobs and tended a huge garden that provided most of their food. They too were rather intimately involved with the Cayce material. Our toddlers used to play together in a big plastic wading pool next to Wendy's coveted strawberry patch.

Sometimes we would sit outside in the cool of the evening, watching brilliant stars appear through the fading yellow-orange and blue of the heavenly canopy. The blazing sky would slowly give birth to lazy, yellow moons that would illuminate the gentle rolling hills. It was not unusual for our conversations to be inter-rupted by the plaintive howling of coyotes echoing from some-where out of the distant shadows. Sometimes there would be a surprise volley of shooting stars streaking across the heavens. All this made the trek over the rutted gravel road more than simply worthwhile.

I remember one Sunday afternoon, just after I completed the setting of the aluminum gate to railroad ties that were used as corner and end posts for the barbed-wire fence that surrounded the property. Sitting quietly in a reflective moment, allowing my-self to enjoy the fatigue of a good day's work, I asked the land to forgive me for the folly of encasing it in wire.

Suspended in contemplation, I felt a gentle placement of an unseen hand upon my left shoulder. A definite, but very subtle whisper of a voice began telling me that soon I would be leaving this place and would not see it again. I was being told by some-one or something that my time in this place was over. It seemed rather strange at the time. It's the kind of thing that makes you wonder if it might just be your imagination, born of physically strenuous work and dehydration.

I remember telling Susan of my encounter and her looking at me rather blankly, shrugging her shoulders, and walking away. But a year later, it all somehow seemed to start making sense.

It took some doing, but we eventually sold our territorial-style, slump-block home, nestled in the outskirts of Tucson. I would miss working with the children in our little vegetable garden, next to the red-brick patio, as well as the early morning jogging along the bike path of the Old Spanish Trail that wound its way so gracefully through the lush Sonoran Desert.

With the suggestion of the Source, we took a preliminary family trip to Telluride. We were guided to a suitable contractor. By the next winter we found ourselves in a modest family home, across from the town park in the heart of the Telluride valley. We still had a bit of decorating to tend to as well as decks and a garage to complete, but we were basically settled.

Decades before, this was the pasture where Dad and his mining partner, Oscar, sometimes kept our horses, as well as caring for a few other mounts. When I was a teenager we employed a Pinto named Billy, a large mare we called Big Red, and a mule that had no name at all. They were used as pack animals when prospecting in the high alpine basins during the summer. But most of the time they were allowed to just roam free. I was delighted when Dad told me that he had bought the Pinto with me in mind.

Susan and I had secured a lot and had somehow been able to build our family home in precisely the same spot where the old barn had once stood. I remembered my encounters with the Pinto, sometimes taking him up Bear Creek as far as the old Wasatch trail. This was an activity that did not have the approval of my rather guarded and protective mother.

Telluride is one of those places that you really can't describe. If you haven't found it yet, you will understand what I mean once you get there. The town first sprouted at the foot of a box canyon that is a few hundred yards wide and a couple of miles long. The town continues to grow, up into the canyons and onto the mesas—waiting, sometimes yearning, for a good scouring from the next ice age. The mountains rise on three sides from an elevation of approximately 8,500 to major promontories of just under 14,000 feet.

It is ringed with granite as well as red-rock cliffs and spires. And, there is always some snow on the peaks even if just in the depths of shadowy crags. To the east, cascading down from high alpine basins, is one of the highest waterfalls in the country. Of course, there is an abundance of evergreen, aspen trees, and flowering meadows.

As the seasons change the valley goes through phases of emerald green, luminescent yellows, flaming oranges and reds—until the arrival of purifying blankets of luminous white snow. The swirling and bouncing San Miguel River runs through the valley floor, eventually making its crystal-clear contribution to the long and muddy Colorado River.

Among the reasons that the Source brought us here was the conviction that this is supposedly one of five major centers within the planet. It was explained that this was a place where many souls first found their way into this earthly realm. This was the apparent explanation for the visions, profound attraction and soulful longing that I had been experiencing; that was drawing me back to this ancient place of beginning and ending.

Susan's mother, Mollie, reluctantly settled into her private parlor on the ground floor. She had her own bathroom, her own entrance, the largest closet in the house and grumbled that she felt like a prisoner because there was no bus service. Our children also had their own rooms and seemed very excited at their good fortune.

The main living area was on the second floor. It sported an adequate kitchen and a great room where the family would convene. On the west end of the second floor was a modest room that was originally designed as a small dining room with a pantry. We decided to use it as an office. With the advent of computers, faxes and FedEx Susan was able to bring her "little business" and most of her court-reporting clients right along with her.

On the east end of the second floor, a series of windows and two large glass doors opened to an upper deck, providing a panoramic view of the spectacular, majestic mountain scenery that towered all around us. There was also a clear view of the city park, which once lay right on the other side of the San Miguel River. The river was a mere two hundred feet away from our door, just on the other side of Colorado Avenue, which we simply called main street.

This was a time just before the park began to be gobbled up by an onslaught of city maintenance buildings, along with an inundation of "necessary public recreational facilities" and the accompanying asphalt parking lots.

Along the alley, I was completing an attached, one-car garage. This is where I had hoped to house the used jeep that had been purchased just for our new adventure. However, neither the jeep nor any other vehicle ever saw the inside of the garage, due to the family custom of needing every inch of anything resembling a garage as a storage room.

In the mid-eighties, real estate in Colorado skiing communities was getting ridiculously expensive. The total cost of the home, along with the move, came to an unbelievably extravagant sum of almost seventy-five thousand dollars. Fortunately, after our wild spending spree, we owned the house outright and still had some meager savings.

The third floor of the home was crafted out of what earlier generations might term the attic. The walls of our roof were angled at about 45 degrees. A little additional headroom and floor space was afforded by the addition of a couple of dormers. On one side of each of two rooms, a four-foot perpendicular wall was constructed that abutted the 45-degree ceiling. The stubby little walls provided some interesting triangular storage space, with short little doors, suitable for toddlers and leprechauns.

When you came to the top of the stairs, the master bedroom was to the right. To the left, was the heart of the home. This room was set aside for sacred ceremony and communion with the creator. It was a place dedicated to prayerful study, the discipline of meditation, and the practice of yoga. Most mornings and often at night, here we would sit; sometimes in awe, sometimes in apprehension of the teachings that would be imparted through this voice, this connection, that was simply referred to as "The Source."

Through the tall, floor-length window you could see up into the sacred promontories looming above the cliff face of the great granite wall of the massive canyon. There, in the East, less than a mile away you could gaze upon the headwaters of the San Miguel River cascading down into the valley from the high mountain basins.

Through the window in the dormer, to the South, you could look upon the crystal waters of a river that the people once recognized as being sacred. Across the way you could look up into Bear Creek Canyon, a place where many initiated souls are homeward bound.

The "channel who speaks" would sit in the West. The "channel who did not speak" would sit in the North.

The Source suggested, and the speaking channel selected, a multi-faceted crystal that was suspended near the top of the window in the East. When the sun would rise, the room would come alive with a myriad of rainbow colors—sometimes still, sometimes twisting and dancing along the white walls of our sacred sanctuary.

The Source suggested, and the channel accepted, that we place a handcrafted clay pot, of our choosing, at the base of the window beneath the radiating crystal. With the vessel at the center we were to divide the space into four quadrants by visualizing an imaginary "X" upon the floor. The space located in the upper left and the lower right was to be my domain. The space in the lower left and upper right was to be Susan's domain.

Each of us was encouraged to place objects in our individual corners that would be reflective or emblematic of our spiritual path. It could be anything: as many or as few items as we wished. Items could be added or removed. It could change and evolve over time, reflecting our evolving interests or focus.

Thus was created a sacred, living shield upon an altar that would reflect the aspirations, inclinations, and needs of both. We were told that this was once the way that it had been done in an ancient and forgotten culture.

Thus was our individualized altar and shield commissioned and sanctified; born of prayer, meditation and clarity of purpose.

Sometimes being gently awakened by Source, we would rise from our slumber and be directed to sit for a reading. This eventually gave birth to a set of recorded and transcribed readings that become known as ...

"SOURCE: We wish to continue with the Teachings of the Land and of the People. This will be also in New Mexico.

You will go in such route: You will go down past Mesa Verde to Durango, past there to Chimney Rock Ruin. Then, go down from Pagosa Springs down through Chama, through Espanola, stopping at all the ruins along the way, which are many. Then to go to Santa Fe, and then to visit through the sites.

For this is the circle, the southern circle of the boomerang, the route.

Then you will go down to Bernalillo where you turn back north, stopping—must stop at Jemez Pueblo.

QUESTIONER: Wait, I didn't understand.

SOURCE: Jemez, as in Spanish. Jemez, J-E-M-E-Z, Jemez Pueblo. And stopping there and coming back up through Nagaeezi and Aztec, to stop at the Aztec National Monument and back through Durango. Go up through Colorado that way through Durango and back to Adnipoche [Telluride].

On the trip also you will be looking each for something for the shield, each separately, to find something with which you will blend. This will be talking, too, about the ancient people who come from Spain, who were in that lifetime born in Spain to come to this world here, to return to their point of origin, to continue the holy sanctification of the area.

And you will be told of many things on this trip. We understand that there will be concern on the financial cost of the trip, but this must not concern you at this time. All will be provided. To open self and to not be concerned, for that which will be imparted will be of great importance to the continuation of this work.

Today we wish that the entity who is the channel who speaks should finish the work that is binding her and to also continue with the transcription of the Colorado National Monument tour, for this will be the continuation upon which the next trip will revolve."

This was an era of many pilgrimages which would take us to dozens of small towns, bustling cities, ancient ruins, geographical features, and sacred sites across the Four Corners region and throughout the Southwest. Under the tutelage of the Source, we would pack our belongings, the children, and Winchester, the family dog, and be down the road for another impromptu adventure.

It was not uncommon for the kids to fail to find much inspiration in the endless hours of driving across the open countryside. Sometimes, they would respond accordingly. These were not always blissful adventures. Sometimes there would be scant communication from the Source. A couple of times we were told that we were being asked to follow difficult energy lines and to engage in prayers or chanting in order to ease anguish that was pouring forth from the earth. Once we were even invited to a California earthquake! It was mild and we survived.

There were times when we did not even know where we would be going. We would just pack and leave. The Source was rather fond of the idea of taking us on long, circular routes that would take in a cluster of experiences. Sometimes it would be for a thousand miles and sometimes just a side trip on our way to nearby towns like Ouray, Montrose, or Grand Junction during a shopping excursion. It could be in any season and in all kinds of weather. Sometimes we would just happen to show up at some pueblo just before the commencement of a ceremony to which we would be subsequently invited.

On one trip, we were asked to stop at the side of the road in order to view a rather nasty cornice on the side of a cliff face with a warning that it was about to graduate to avalanche status. We were dumbfounded when we discovered that folks in the other two vehicles had also been guided by their "source" so we could all witness our arrival at the same location at precisely the same time.

We were so stunned that, when the avalanche cut loose, we all got back in our cars and left; not thinking to exchange names, phone numbers, or addresses. The Source proclaimed that that was not necessary. And, it was best for each of the three "speaking channels" to follow their own paths and make their own discoveries. This was just one of several events orchestrated by the Source along with one of its favorite admonitions "Lest ye doubt."

The Source generally took a rather authoritarian stance. If the instructions were questioned, we would be reminded that it was ever our choice to respond or not. On occasion, in a spirit of cooperation, a pilgrimage would be postponed or adjusted "to accommodate the ongoing needs of the entities." It was explained that there were other channels who were also given an opportunity to participate in a similar path, but over time had fallen away.

We were also reminded that this had been a personal contract and commitment that we had made long before we were born into this present lifetime. The whole process eventually became something that you had to feel inside yourself and to trust. It was not something that was necessarily open to the introspection of mind in its attempt to make everything rational.

During those times when the Source did not seem to be present and there were no expeditions in the offering, we wondered if somehow we had missed something or had not appropriately responded. However, the Source always seemed to emerge once more. Often, communication would not be available when you wanted it, but would show up totally unexpected, sometimes with messages you really didn't want to hear.

In general, the Source seemed pleased with our level of cooperation. As time went on, it became more and more of an informal presence, never knowing when it might come through to provide a bit of advice on diet, health or child care. It was becoming an integral partner and companion, an intimate part of our daily lives; sometimes a bit perplexing, but mostly a very welcomed visitor.

So, here, from a small loft within the sacred valley, was a glorious platform of potential, a launching pad for a great adventure, a place where the many paths had become one and would separate and become many before returning to one path once more. A place from which the word would go forth in times, ways, and places that would be impossible for us to ignore; in ways that would astonish us beyond our wildest expectations and our most vivid imagination.

Chapter 6

On Mediumship and Channeling

W hether you are a casual observer or an astute and experienced investigator, it is quite easy to become both fascinated and baffled by the multitude of practices that all seem to come under the heading of "channeling."

For most people who have had the opportunity to observe or to become involved in the phenomena of channeling or mediumship, there is an almost inevitable question which will arise. At some point the thoughtful person just has to wonder what or who is speaking and by what authority or authenticity does it present itself. A coherent analysis or elucidation is generally hampered by the fact that the terminology used to describe these goings on is mostly inept, or evolving and transitory.

What I mean by that, is that the terminology is mostly vague or inadequate, and thereby misleading. The words we use change over time in the ever-evolving quest to describe the ways that the phenomenon tends to shift from place to place and from time to

63

time, and in its manner and form of presentation. It is often too easy to make simplistic and erroneous assumptions.

This elusive and mostly inspiring phenomenon is nothing new. It has been going on for millennia and will undoubtedly continue well into the future. It will evolve and change as our insight and understanding of these manifestations continues to evolve and adjust to our most recently crafted insights— even though much of the time we are mostly trying to be clearer and more concise about the same issues, over and over again.

Dissention between what is channeling and what is mediumship is often distorted or obfuscated by the fact that certain groups of people, because of their personal exposure and involvement, tend to cluster around certain types of phenomena and develop a rather protective, assuming posture—believing that what they have experienced is the truest and purest, most reliable and most useful, way that these forces, energies, or spirits would manifest.

The truth is, we mostly trust and value that with which we have the most experience, and have therefore become the most comfortable. This is true whether it be our own particular brand of organized religion, or the so-called newly-aged, and predominately unorganized and unrefined manifestations of that which many like to label as spiritualism.

Still, I believe there are certain elements and patterns of these manifestations that can generally be observed and recognized, which will offer some clarifying insights.

Channeling is the word that I tend to use as meaning the highest, or most pure, though not always the most useful, process by which communication is received. It is as if there is a single, combined source of conscious awareness that pervades all of time, space, and possibility.

This "Source," which some prefer to call God, seems to have the ability to reach into the psyche of a single individual and express through the spoken word the inspired concepts and information that individuals and groups will often gather around to ponder (to study) in order to receive the benefit of that which is imparted. More often than not, for better or for worse, it becomes a cult. If it survives, it may become a religion.

Sometimes, it would seem that truly channeled information is like an impersonal computer that responds to the questions or needs of the petitioners, even when it seems they are unable to form concise and meaningful questions for themselves.

At other times, this phenomenon seems to be more like a freely moving single point of consciousness, or entity, that moves from place to place, mind to mind, soul to soul. And is capable of and willing to communicate experiences and information through a channel, to a place of more limited consciousness for those who could not otherwise be capable of communing with other realms of existence.

Although ostensibly of one unified source, it apparently has the capacity to manifest in ways that would best meet the needs of those to whom it speaks. Being a bit vague and abstract, difficult for us to comprehend, it can seemingly manifest at will as a certain aspect or archetype of itself by becoming individualized as an angel, kachina, or other entity or spirit.

At other times, it would seem that individual souls and spirit beings of endless varieties are all loosely associated in some sort of borderless and interactive universe, again presumably of one unified, all-encompassing force or energy. And, from time to time, it is possible that these are somehow brought forth to commune with those of us who have a mere temporal, and consequently more limited, earthly existence.

At the other pole of this continuum, seemingly opposite from channeling of the unified, all-pervading source of conscious energy is what I call the mediumship experience.

In mediumship, it is as if (and perhaps in fact), another entity, person, or spirit inhabits the existing physical body of another person. The medium seems to give up their body whether voluntarily or involuntarily to something or someone else, who comes from another plane of existence, to visit us in this worldly realm in which we currently find ourselves.

Channeling, to me, is more replete with guidance and teachings from the highest, or most knowledgeable and benevolent states of existence. A medium, however, may simply be a person temporarily inhabited by the soul or spirit of your grandfather, and who may not understand or know any more than you do.

If your grandfather were an enlightened being, or if you always benefited from his presence and savored his council, then this is fine. However, the truth is, his presence or counsel may not be any better or worse than anyone else that you may happen to be hanging out with, whether on this plane or the next. Just because someone is dead or has lost their earthly body doesn't mean they have suddenly become smart or wise.

However, it can become quite convincing if a medium, who never met your deceased grandfather, suddenly starts using his same mannerisms and/or patterns of speaking and has intimate knowledge of your time together on earth. This can be a profoundly impressive way to affirm personal proof for survival of the spirit after the physical death.

It may be possible to resolve psychological and emotional trauma, to be able to say last words, resolve misunderstandings, and receive good wishes and blessings if you happen to have the opportunity to converse with what you undeniably believe is your deceased relative.

But, maybe you don't simply get your esteemed grandfather. What if you get to talk to Freud, Ghandi, Alexander the Great, Moses, Elijah, Mother Mary, Mohammad, Jesus, or an angel sent from God, the most high? At what point is it mediumship and at what point is it channeling?

To me, the difference between channeling and mediumship is in the manifestation of universal consciousness as opposed to the manifestation of individual consciousness. Although, in fact, there does appear to be a continuum or progression of spirit and spirits that can manifest from an infinite as well as from a finite perspective.

And, there is still something else to consider. What if there were no survival after death, but somehow the constellation of energy, the thought patterns of each one who has ever lived is somehow still out there in the universe, like the fading image of an exploded star that in reality no longer exists.

Perhaps a medium, or channel if you prefer, whether unknowlingly or consciously has the capability to take on that energy like a program being played in a computer, thus *acting* like the person who no longer exists on any plane and *saying* the things that they would say if they still existed.

There is also the prospect that different personalities and individuals may spring from inside ourselves, not from some other source, but from different aspects of the same self, in much the same manner as a single person can be very different—different attitudes, different interests and goals at different, times, stages, or ages—in a single lifetime.

Consider what it might be like to meet yourself at ten, or forty, or eighty. You may always be the same person, yet have a very different presentation depending on the point in time and therefore appearing as a series of ever-evolving snapshots of the same soul with changing parts of the personality; yet, at the core you are always the same being, the same individual.

Perhaps when the Source speaks, it is merely that most distant, but most aware and alive part of our own individual soul that is always in the presence of whatever universal force or godhead that there may be. Perhaps it is something that we get tapped into that responds when the need is great and when some allegedly more intelligent and wise consciousness somehow knows the time and place that is right for such expression.

In addition to the categories of channeling and mediumship comes my third category, which I simply bundle together as psychic gifts—gifts or abilities that do not require taking on or being inhabited by some alternate spirit beings or personalities. One "simply" sees, hears, feels, tastes, smells, or otherwise intuits and becomes cognizant of situations and events through the usual senses, but from somewhere beyond the immediate time and space that most of us are perceiving.

These can generally fall into categories such as clairvoyance, clairaudience, clairsentience, etc. But these individuals don't seem to have a change in their personality, voice, or mannerisms. They essentially continue to be who they are during the experience; though it is not uncommon for those who purport to have visions or hear voices, or to have spirit guides, to receive words, insights, and suggestions that they pass onto others who may come seeking counsel.

These practitioners often use as much of their own skill as they use assistance from that which we might call otherworldly forces. These I would refer to as psychics, not channels or mediums; though in these times channels often have the capacity to be a combination of psychic, medium and/or channel.

I have always found it curious that almost all of these practitioners prefer to see themselves as channels, rather than as mediums. It seems there is something uplifting about channeling and something a bit pejorative about "merely" being involved in mediumship.

The possibilities for the conscious mind to ponder seem to be endless and unsolvable, yet their implications can be far reaching and profound.

Most of us just eventually give up and accept by faith what is true or not true. What we decide to believe is all too often based on what is easy and comfortable rather than what is true. I personally take it on faith that the pursuit of what is true is worth the effort.

Experience has shown me that, eventually, one has to discover and develop the awareness of a different kind of mind and a different kind of knowing: a different type of vehicle of consciousness that the soul might use in its endless journeys through many places, planes, and types of experiences.

At some point, the conscious mind becomes clumsy and inept and the necessity of allowing this different kind of mind arises. This is not merely a feeling or emotional mind, but an intuitive mind. It is a spirit mind, if you will, that can take in impressions, sensations, thoughts, and feelings, but not merely indulge in emotional feelings alone.

The idea of going for what you feel, because it is from the heart and allegedly superior, can be quire troubling for many; it borders on believing if it feels good do it, if not don't. Again, this is not merely an emotional feeling, but rather more of an intuitive knowing, which may or may not include an accompanying emotional feeling.

In all this, the best advice that might be given is "Ye shall know them by their fruits." However, even then you have to come to some conclusion of judgment regarding the usefulness as well as the validity of the fruit. It is not always clear and obvious.

So discernment is always the key. And discernment can take a lot of time and patience, but it is well worth the effort because, in the end, it is all you have. Upon this we shall evolve or perish. Somehow I have developed a belief that all sincere efforts are hopefully acceptable and shall eventually be rewarded.

What I can testify to from my own experience is that these experiences are as real as any of the experiences that human beings have. And their implications are just as far reaching, if not more so, than the everyday, usual physical sensations and experiences that we share with one another.

Again, if any of this stuff is true, we are supposedly evolving. Whether we are observing these phenomena from without or

from within, we all have a decision or judgment to make: to ignore the whole subject and its potential blessings and insights or
to simply gobble down the whole thing without much rational
thought of what may really be going on.

A third alternative is to attempt to winnow away the grain
from the chaff, lest we remain ignorant and unaware of the essential nature of what it means to be a soul engrossed in a
human experience.

In common discussion, the concept of channeling has become such a catchall that it can mean almost anything and usually does mean just about anything. Even casual observers will
soon become acutely aware of the multitude of self-deluded and
slightly deranged folks who come to believe that whatever happens to pop into their heads is something channeled from a spirit
being or divine source. It can be easy to begin to wonder, suspect,
and then pretend that you are being touched by something extraordinary when it is nothing more than the machinations of
your own imagination.

There is an exercise that psychotherapists sometimes em-
ploy to act out conflict or ambivalence in the quest for clarity and
reunification. Many simply refer to it as a "chair exercise." In
this process an individual can sit in a chair, facing another chair.
While sitting in one chair, the participant may take on a role of
expressing their quandary, a problem, or an issue to resolve.

The protagonist, after stating his dilemma in whatever simplistic or eloquent terms the individual is most comfortable
with, is encouraged to rise and move to another chair and assume the role of advisor or problem solver. Sometimes a third or
fourth chair can be entered into the arena.

Soon, with sufficient encouragement, a person may be observed moving from chair to chair and having a conversation

with him- or herself, which under the right circumstances can end with a plan or resolution. The process with proper coaching can be quite productive.

I have always found this internal role-playing process to be fascinating. One can take upon oneself one role, that of being weak, confused, and powerless. Then, in another chair, one might assume the role of the competent, confident, and patient one; thus releasing an effective and relentless problem solver with a faith that believes that anything is possible.

By this artificial shifting of roles and attitudes one can discover and bring to reality insights and opportunities which otherwise may not have been conscious choices.

If you are stuck, it might be possible to use this process to decide if you should really buy that new Harley. In the first chair, you know you want it. Life is short and you should allow yourself the joy of owning it.

In the other chair, you might decide it was really too expensive, too impractical. You could buy a new car for the same money. Perhaps the money could best be used for others, not for your own selfish desires. It is dangerous. You could get killed, or even worse become maimed and crippled.

In a third chair, it is not uncommon to discover the emergence of the role of a wise and helpful mediator who, given the chance, can be fair and amazingly ingenious in getting the two opposing sides into agreement—resolution.

Depending on the level of sincerity and the subject at hand, a lot of great stuff can come out: revealing and healing old hurts, assumptions, and barriers that one did not even realize were there. Again, issues and possibilities are revealed, options and solutions can become more obvious.

Yet all of these "personages" are of the same individual. However, it has been this writer's observation that some will actually grab hold of this phenomena, almost as if taking upon themselves a mantle of what they would suppose their spirit guides, angels, or Jesus might say to them about this or that, actually believing they are channeling other entities.

It can be quite fascinating to observe in oneself how a sense of peace, confidence, and an improved quality of advice can begin to come forth as we assume and seek the highest that may be within us.

Some will even encourage and teach others to involve themselves in this process, or a similar one, in the quest to develop the ability to actually become a psychic, channel, or medium. And it may even aid in that purpose.

But I would like to make one thing as clear as possible. Although many may become fascinated and delight in this process, this is not anywhere close to the quality or level of what is happening when spirit quickens a prepared vessel and the words of the divine pour forth. And, even here, from time to time, will come the distortions or the imprinting, if you will, of the individual characteristics of the personality through which the divine energies flow.

Though certainly such exercises have their value, it is as the difference between that which is a parlor trick and that which is the legitimate fruit of the divinely inspired. I personally believe it is usually preferable to allow the opening to occur by surrendering through faith and trust rather than to attempt the forcing of the opening through a corrupted ego, which can distort and obfuscate any sense of authenticity.

As yet there has been no mention of the dark side. Beware. There is one. Just as there is that in this earthly realm that would take from you and wish you ill; so, on the other planes of existence lie those beings, which may be of that which you would not want to experience.

But the pure in heart, or even those who would in sincerity simply hope within the purity of their intent, have no need of concern of such. For evil is most often successful only when there is a corrupted intent. But, then who among us is perfect?

The best defense is always the purity of purpose by which you walk the path that has been placed before you. Though innocence may be crucified, it shall rise again and again and never be truly defeated. Again, for me, this has become a thing of faith, but I do most sincerely believe it is true.

This elucidation would not be complete without the mention of what might be termed the natural channel. This is the highest form that the true seeker would find: That as you go about the activities of the daily life, here and there you would be subtly, gently quickened to say this or that, to do this or that, to realize this or that. This is the true partnership that we would have grow within thee to deliver the messiah of your own temple into the earth where you yet reside.

I am not going to talk much about the charlatans and the self-deluded. It is widely known and accepted that this is a part of the mix within mystical arenas. I wish to address the genuine experience.

There is an ancient tradition among some learned masters that a student will not be taught if he has to be *convinced* that God exits or that the pursuit of same has some intrinsic value. The purpose of mentored teaching and practices is presumably to be able to recognize, manifest, or possibly merge with that which some of us like to call God.

Recently, many of us prefer to call it "the universe." It has fewer connotations and bad memories from the religious dogmas and organizations, which some find objectionable. But it seems to me that God is God regardless of the wrapper, or how well or how mistakenly you imagine or judge it.

It you don't accept that something is divine, or that divinity is even possible, then you are most likely not yet ready for esoteric instruction and will most likely be unable to accept its value. You are best left to meander through the labyrinth of mundane human endeavor until you come to some inescapable revelation through your own experience that there is something more. At some point you will come to know that this is all important.

Most will long to commune with the source of our creation as fully as may be possible. Some will become terrified at the mere prospect of its existence and will even spend their lives struggling relentlessly, hoping to prove to the world but mostly to themselves that nothing of value exists beyond the narrow limitations of our earthly experience. They struggle valiantly because at their core they know it is real, and they fear it intensely.

Beyond the charlatans and our own self-delusions there is something out (or in) there that wishes us well and is trying to reach us. Beyond all the parlor games, silliness, and marketing to the gullible for profit, there is an incontrovertible reality. It is indescribable and profound. Some of us seem burdened or graced with the task of trying to describe it anyway. Perhaps a fool's errand; but I think not.

Ultimately, you *will* decide for yourself. As you choose, so shall your path be made. Most tend to judge quickly, to either dismiss the idea as folly or to blindly embrace whatever is offered to them. A few will attempt a middle path to attempt to apply discernment or to carefully anazlyze and intuit. This is all well and good.

However, when the subject in question becomes your spouse and partner, the mother of your children, it all takes on a rather different perspective. It is no longer just a curious and possibly intriguing concept. It becomes alive in the flesh, in your face, right before you. And, though others may question the authenticity of the experience, when you are right there day after day, the reality of this phenomenon, regardless of your immediate or eventual judgment, you know it is very real; it is much, much more real than what any supposition or analysis might render.

There is something here. I know it is real because I have lived it. This presence, this Source has been here since the beginning. It comes again and again to awaken and enliven the consciousness of humankind to remind us that there truly is something divine. It is a part of us. It lives all around us and inside of us—whether we know it or not, whether we understand it or not. And, most likely it is beyond the ability of the conscious mind to fully comprehend. But that should never stop us from trying.

In this time and place, just like in times of old from whence the sacred scriptures came, channeling and mediumship have once again become the tools of revelations and ascension. And, just like the green sprouts of spring burgeoning forth out of fertile earth, in this time and place, so-called channeling, mediumship, and psychic gifts continue to burst forth everywhere.

There are those who would say that all of these expressions are evil and not what a true seeker should partake of. However, you might rethink that perspective. For if that were so, how would anyone ever hear the words of the prophets or the messages of the angels.

Of course, the easiest stance to take is that all of this is delusion and does not exist in reality, but rather is born of pure imagination. There will always be those who maintain that the world is flat regardless of the uncomfortable evidence to the contrary.

It is as if spirit is forcing itself through recalcitrant flesh to announce the advent of our resurrection. It will change, evolve, mutate, disappear, and reappear as the human spirit draws ever nearer to its origin and its destiny; it will take on whatever form or process is required until it reaches its fullness in its time and place of completion.

So who or what is the Source of the channeled information that came through Susan?

What follows is an excerpt of a transcript of a recorded conversation with the Source answering the question.

(The author was the "Questioner." The "Channel" was his wife. The "Source" was the source of the readings.)

"QUESTIONER: I'm wondering who's speaking during this. I mean, it's like my impression is the Source can be a lot of enlightened Masters, the Angelic Host, or Jesus as the Christ, and others, all speaking in unison, or one speaking at a time.

I just get the impression that the Source at this time is taking on what I've said before is more like a guru-chela relationship. I'm wondering if it's a variety of energies and manifestations and personalities, or if it's Jesus or an old Hopi medicine man, or what are we drawing upon by these experiences as we go around to these points?

SOURCE: These are as the entity would understand as the Christed individuals who have become as merged with the higher consciousness, yet still as influenced during the communication by personality, yet responding to the needs of the entities to whom it would communicate, to raise that level even within the earth plane, and that is diminished, so does it raise the consciousness literally of all who would respond, whether consciously or not, within the earth plane now presently in embodiment.

So that the nature of this Source is the higher consciousness of man looking into the duality that still exists here [earthly existence], from the oneness; that it would communicate; that it would make the days, make the transition as lighter, as less burdensome in the times to come.

CHANNEL: Does that answer your question?

QUESTIONER: Somewhat. From this perspective that I am in, I don't know if it would be appropriate to ask for anything more specific or not. So, I guess I have to leave it up to your judgment.

SOURCE: Here we see that the entity already understands the nature of that which has been given.

CHANNEL: So, what is being said is that it is the higher consciousness, but yet there is still personality.

QUESTIONER: It's a conglomerate, orchestrated by one universal Source?

SOURCE: Yes. Yes.

QUESTIONER: And they might talk as one or they might have one or two come in that have expertise in an area or an interest, or whatever, and one at the same time or both - -

CHANNEL: Responding to the needs, whatever is there.

QUESTIONER: I don't know if that means that just because this communication is happening, it makes it easier for everybody on some psychic level, or if it is that over decades there's hundreds of people doing this [psychic channeling], and even though people may not agree with it or believe it or accept it, at least these ideas are around and become part of the culture, so that it makes the whole overall thought form of man's consciousness a little more in tune with the infinite, so that the shock to the conscious mind which we might be coming through during the transition isn't quite as strong or shattering.

SOURCE: Although, as has been given, in previous times of embodiment, in the ancient times that man was as in constant communication with the divine, so it is the return to this nature, to the acceptance of the truth of this—of this capacity within man, that he may return to it; that he may not seek the leadership and guidance of that—of that mundane level which would lead him astray [misguided religious doctrine] from that which he truly seeks, but to again interconnect with that network which is of the higher interconnect with that network which is of the higher consciousness in which there can be no falsehoods."

Chapter 7

The Emergence of Hawk Woman

I t happened on one of those long pilgrimages that sent us deep into the Four Corners area of the great Southwest. I would drive. The kids rode in the backseat. Susan would be sitting to my right. Winchester would lie on his blanket, on top of the luggage in the rear compartment of our 1979 International Scout. Sometimes we would all sing together and our furry friend would launch into a serenade of mournful howling that brought much laughter and delight.

Mollie, my mother-in-law, was very happy to remain at home in Telluride. With her advancing years, travel was becoming difficult for her. She enjoyed having the house to herself. Frankly, we all enjoyed having a break from her. Years later, we would realize that she was having early bouts of Alzhiemer's disease. The Source claimed that this was the path that the entity had chosen. And, that at the soul level, she had actually benefited from the experience. However, it was one of those things that "did not have to have been."

We were driving along somewhere in the Navajo Nation. I think it was just south of Kayenta in Northern Arizona. Susan had learned to carry a small, but good quality tape recorder in her purse. As we traveled, the Source would intermittently impart information. When she could feel the presence, and knew the Source was about to speak, the channel would grasp the recorder with both hands and hold it close to her chest; thus the dialogue between the Source and the channels could be recorded.

More and more information was coming in a conversational format. By that time, the channeled voice that emanated from Susan was beginning to sound more like her normal speaking voice. However, it still came through with its distinctive cadence and tone. It was not uncommon for the Source to break into our conversations, as well as initiate a conversation with us. It was becoming ever clearer that whatever this Source was, it was always present.

Topics would range from the sublime to the mundane: describing ancient civilizations, commenting on newly developing technology, including political and social observations, perhaps suggesting another change in diet, or offering recommendations for child care or even recommending a particular restaurant or motel. Often, there were critical reasons why we needed to be at certain places at certain times. Sometimes there were explanations and sometimes not.

Over the years, we did note that we were able to avoid some very troublesome storms, traffic calamities, and even natural disasters. Other times, we were brought right into the midst of danger because somehow the presence of a "conscious channel" at a particular time and place could mediate difficulties that others were about to experience. Of course, these episodes could also ostensibly contribute to our own growth and edification.

As we traveled through Indian country, we had been receiving teachings on how souls were first attracted into physical bodies. It seems that at one time some of us were as pure spirit, without a body or any particular physical form. As we moved about the universe, we began to explore different dimensions and levels of consciousness as well as material creations. Some of us apparently became interested in, and attended to, a place that we later came to call planet Earth.

In the beginning, we would wonder what it might be like to drift as the wind, flow in the water, become alive in fire, or to simply lie within dense earth. We observed and explored this multi-verse of physical sensation with great curiosity and wonder. Some of us began to linger, wanting to experience even more intimately what it would be like to fly through the air, swim in the sea, or walk upon the land.

In time, we learned how to project ourselves into the earth at will, in order to experience all these things. We became accustomed to occupying these elemental, animal, plant, and earth creations and delighted in the novelty of these diverse feelings and sensations. As time continued, we began to merge into these attractions that had become our preferred or favored experiences; thus we became more and more individualized, fragmented, and separated from our original point of pristine, unified consciousness.

We were told that our presence even began to influence how plant and animal life might be created and mutated, reflecting our attitudes and interests. Some groups even participated in how land masses and geologic formations would be created, uplifted, and eroded, even to the extent of creating the various forms, curious shapes, and oddities that still fascinate us in places like Arches and Canyon Lands, which emerged out of the earth in a place we now call Utah.

After eons of time and experience, but all too soon, as some would say, we began to forget from whence we had come. It was like today; when we go to a movie, watch television, or become engrossed in a book, we tend to lose ourselves. By paying attention and focusing intently on something, we can become mesmerized by the story before us. For awhile, we can forget who and where we are. While becoming engrossed and focused on another world impacted by our own thoughts and ways of perceiving, we forget about the world we have come from, leaving it far behind until something shakes us from our dream-like slumber and we begin to remember from whence we came.

Eventually we awaken from our entertainment, walk out of the theatre, or close the book and return back home to our usual state of consciousness and awareness. But for the moment we were transported to other times, places, and experiences with alternative ways of thinking, emoting, and being.

Eventually we became so enamored and entrapped in this earth experience that we became bound to it. Many of us bit deeply into this earthly realm and became lost, deaf and blind; ignorant of our heritage of spirit from whence we had fallen.

Though we existed and had our experience within the minerals, plants, and animals, we had no bodies of our own in order to live, move, and have our being upon the face of our newly forming earthly home. So, the momentum continued. And, responding to our intentions, flesh bodies rose up reflecting our needs and interests. As the breath of life was breathed into them, these newly evolved bodies became living souls; spirit that could live within a custom-designed, earthly wrapper and move about within a three-dimensional plane.

The Source explained that this is how much of our ancestral and Native American lore and ceremonies originated. It is the soul's memory recalling and reliving these ancient experiences. So, man, now in his current body, still remembers and pays homage to those ancient times when his spirit first co-mingled into the earth; when he actually lived within the many mineral, plant, and animal kingdoms.

Holy men and women, shamans all, can still sense, remember, and use these energies in limited ways to quicken the spirit, to render ancient teachings, and to experience different ways of communing and being—even recalling ancient insights into the ways of prophecy and arcane healing.

All of this Source-inspired thought was taking a bit of time to assimilate and digest. Some of it I had heard before and it did explain some of the experiences I had been having on the mountain in Telluride. But it was time for a break. So the Source had withdrawn a while and was affording us some intellectual "down time" as we bounced along through the pinks, reds, and purples of the desert landscape around us.

🐦 🐦 🐦

Then, it happened. I was so startled I almost ran off the road with my heart pounding as Susan's shrieks echoed in my ears. She had spontaneously erupted from out of a trance-like slumber with great enthusiasm and shouting.

"I'm here! I can see! I'm flying inside the bird! I can remember!"

I don't recall the exact words, but it was fairly close to that. She started gasping for air and shaking, almost like a panic attack. After settling down she began to explain. Soon the Source chimed in and at some point we engaged the tape recorder.

She explained that, for lack of a better contemporary name, she had been called Hawk Woman. With the assistance of the Source, the channel was looking back and recovering a memory from her original, first lifetime in the earth. She was a founding soul of the tradition of the Hawk Clan, one of the many bird clans that have been handed down in legend, parable, and ceremonial lore. Her kind was why we sometimes envision our angels with wings, interacting between the heavenly and earthly realms.

It was explained that during this first incarnation, the entity (Susan) was more spirit than flesh and capable of leaving her body and flying at will with the hawks and up into the universe from which she had originally come. At one time she had lived in the periphery of what eventually became the Hopi-Orabi center. Then she settled into the Utah Canyon Lands region where ancient temples can still be seen. This was a time before the great migrations that are described in Hopi legend and tradition. It was supposedly a time when the level of intuition and presence of spirit was stronger than what most of our modern minds are able to comprehend.

As we approached the San Francisco Peaks outside of Flagstaff, she began speaking in an unknown language and then began chanting. She was consciously remembering and participating in an ancient ceremony, actively remembering the birth of her people upon the meridians from whence the mountains sprang.

After awhile the chanting stopped. Susan returned. We rode along in silence in a state of bliss and awe while the children lay asleep in the backseat, with the dog eyeing us warily.

I remember a subsequent pilgrimage. It was a chilly spring morning. The sky was clear and the sun bright. We were packed and taking a quick look around for any remaining items before we checked out of the motel. Susan was walking in front of me. She began walking slowly, moving more deliberately; then she stopped.

I knew immediately that something was up. My skin was tingling. It felt like my hair was standing on end. Her head bobbed abruptly, but gracefully from side to side. She turned toward me and froze, looking at me intensely; surprised, but trying not to let it show. There was a guttural sound from deep in her throat.

Then Susan said, "Where am I? What happened?"

After a moment the familiar sound and demeanor of the Source chimed in. I remember the words.

"This will be allowed; for it is all a part of the process of re-unification that this one is to endure."

This Hawk Woman had again briefly manifested. Again, it was Susan, in her first incarnation in the flesh. Hawk Woman, while exploring one of her shamanic trances, had stumbled upon herself in a time and place far, far into her distant future. We didn't quite know what to do with this visitor. But she was here, and hopefully to be as an honored guest.

In the beginning, she did not come often and did not stay long. But she periodically looked in upon us and our progress. At first, I would sometimes find her sitting in the meditation room making low vowel sounds that sounded like cooing. Sometimes she would screech. I don't know how these sounds came out of Susan's mouth, but I swear by God's holy prophets that they did.

The Source explained that she was making sounds meant to cleanse our home and in general sanctify the surrounding environment. Years later, I was to discover a group of people who would stand in a circle and make many of these sounds. They called it "intoning." They too described this ritual as a meditative healing process for the earth and all those present.

Hawk Woman was learning to become comfortable with the body (that's Susan's body) so she could eventually learn to talk. Apparently, speech was not used much during her time because the intuitive nature was still so strong that it was seldom necessary.

When Hawk Woman was present, the transformation was incredible. Her lips would slightly purse, resembling a beak. Her movements were abrupt and quick, resembling the movements of a bird. Her eyes blinked blankly and stared, looking as if they were not focusing on anything in particular. There was a tendency for one eye to be slightly crossed. The head would snap back and forth and up and down, as if to constantly survey her environment.

One day, I found myself wondering out loud what she would do if she encountered one of the mice that we were attempting to extricate from our house. She looked at me very sternly as if she were seriously insulted.

I would describe her countenance as severe; no nonsense, intense, assuming she was in charge. She seemed very interested in me. She would sometimes look confused as if she had questions and didn't know how to ask; or perhaps, she didn't understand why I seemed unable to respond.

Eventually, it was learned that she had brought with her a serious problem. This was something that I was to help her with. You see, she had absolutely no sense of humor. She would try, but just couldn't get it. She could keep us in stitches watching her cackle away, trying to learn how to laugh and looking inquisitively at our amused reactions, but not quite being able to comprehend those responses.

In time, she would understand and learn to poke fun at her own pompous nature. She liked to call herself, "the Feathered Presence." I, supposedly being of the jaguar clan, became affectionately known as "Pussycat," a designation that I did not find all that fitting, until I had a smattering of my own experiences.

Most of the time Susan was able to be present enough to be aware of "the old bird" as I sometimes called her. At times, Susan found the whole event hysterically funny. Hawk Woman would do something amusing. Susan would "pop out" (as the expression came to be known in the family) and laugh hysterically. Then, Hawk Woman would "pop back" looking perplexed and insulted.

As the Feathered Presence continued to look in on us, we became more comfortable with each other. Eventually, she became a member of the family who seemed to be able to come and go at will: sometimes coming with a message but mostly coming to observe and learn, not so much to impart.

And, all the while was the constant, patient, informative, and reassuring presence of the Source, helping us all through this process which at times became more than a little unsettling. Somehow the kids took it all in stride. Perhaps it all seemed normal because they didn't know anything else.

This channel had definitely developed an expanded capacity to also be a medium. But, this particular medium was supposedly exhibiting her own self, both from an alternate realm, and within another lifetime.

Meanwhile, the "normal" episodic contact with the Source continued, complete with teachings and pilgrimages. Hawk Woman would sometimes join us on the pilgrimages, occasionally offering a bit of her own teachings and memories. As time went on, her presentation became more human. Eventually, it all began to seem quite normal. We would miss her if we did not hear from her for a few weeks.

Ben, my son, and I were quite active in Boy Scouts. I remember making plans to go to a regional fall rendezvous that had a Mountain Man theme. Some of the participants would set up targets and have tomahawk throwing contests. Usually they were just referred to as hawk throwing contests.

One day the Feathered Presence emerged and became highly incensed about this hawk throwing activity. She held us spellbound for a moment, not knowing what she was going to do or what would happen. Then, she started laughing with great delight. It seems she finally got us. It was obvious that she had finally grasped the idea of humor and joyful laughter.

She disliked the giant windmills that were being erected for the generation of electricity. To her, the propellers looked like wings flailing about with no sensible purpose. She told us there was energy all around us so why would we have to do such a thing "to get this electricity." She was dumbfounded and incredulous. To her, this was the most ridiculous thing that man had ever done throughout all the ages.

I suspect that at least part of her reaction was because she assumed that someone was somehow making fun of her wings. She once told us how painful it was to recall how she and her clan lost their wings as they bit into the earth and became bound to it. I initially assumed this was a metaphor; but I sometimes wonder, given the chronic, bilateral intra-scapular pain that Susan endured.

Eventually, Hawk Woman's tragic story was revealed to us. It was the story of a great betrayal and the loss of innocence. It was her "original sin."

She was among the first of her clan: a healer and a teacher. However, at a critical point, she lacked faith and doubted herself, her abilities, and her creator's wisdom and protection, thus accepting a cleverly crafted deception.

In that ancient time the entity had given birth to several children. This was something that had made her exceedingly proud as she was fulfilling a part of what she understood to be her god-given mandate: to go forth and to multiply, to bring into existence the physical bodies and serve the emerging generations, all waiting to gain entry from the great realms of spirit.

There had been a deceitful rival from before that first incarnation, from a time within the spirit world, from before the progression of souls into this earthly existence. This nemesis followed her, also coming into this realm of flesh. Thus was the duality born into the earth; thus the heavenly battles continue in three-dimensional form. As above; so below.

Hawk Woman had been invited to visit a contiguous region to help teach and inspire those who were beginning to forget their origins—those who could no longer remember who they were and where they came from. They had no teachings. Teaching was also a part of her divine purpose as a member of the compassionate heart of the Hawk Mother, of which she was representative and a part.

Hawk Woman had been told by this nemesis that her children had all been killed in a conflict between the clans. They had been massacred while she was away trying to minister unto the neighboring people.

This made Hawk Woman feel particularly guilty and responsible. How could she have abandoned her own children and left them so vulnerable to go tend to the needs of strangers, rather than being available to care for and protect her own? She felt she was being punished for being so arrogant as to be seduced into believing she could help others. She reasoned that she should have stayed home and cared for her own children and the needs of her own clan.

Subsequently, she spent much of her time in seclusion, mourning and feeling that she had failed both her children and her mandate from the universal Source. This betrayal, the greatest betrayal of all—the betrayal of self by self—left her brooding, sullen, isolated, and alone.

During our associations with this Hawk Woman there was an eventual revealing. For, in fact, the children were still alive and were fully grown, replete with grandchildren. They had been taken away to a hidden place for safety. They were taught wonderful stories of their mother, as one of the matriarchs who had begun their clan. There had been a prophecy that someday she would come back to them. It turned out that it was Hawk Woman's "Pussycat," who found her children and was instrumental in having them reunited.

Again, the "original sin," that sense of shame and guilt, came from her self betrayal, for she blithely believed what she had been told. She had forsaken the use of her own inner knowledge and talents in which she could have sensed, at any time, that her children had been kidnapped and hidden: not murdered. She could have easily found them herself had she simply asked and trusted the guidance that was hers to receive.

However, her lack of faith in the creator and her assumption that what she had been told was correct, corrupted her connection with the infinite. It became eternally difficult for her to come to terms with how she had allowed herself to be so easily fooled, so she continued to plunge into the depths of despair because of a falsehood that could have been easily dispelled. She needed to have her story told and then to discover how to forgive herself.

This reunification was a very soulful and joyous event. It was a time of great healing for the old bird. But for now, as was to be the path for all of us, she had bit into the essence of earth and its separation from pristine spirit. Her journey into the dense earth was complete. It would require a journey of many generations, many lifetimes to be able to reclaim her birthright and be resurrected back into the spirit from whence we all emerged.

Now she watches over all her children as Hawk Mother. She watches each succeeding generation of her incarnating soul that springs forth from her spirit body. She is also of those who are immutably linked to the Great Mother of all who watches over all the children of spirit currently exploring the human domain.

She gives birth to the prophets, messiahs, and saviors of all the ages regardless of the particular culture or historical rendition through which they may emerge. This Hawk Woman, who became a Hawk Mother, is linked as a handmaiden to our great Mother Mary who gives birth over and over again, offering us the blessing and grace of salvation in order to return from the realm of flesh back to the realm of spirit from whence all human souls originate.

After her time with us, the "old bird" could easily laugh at herself. She had forgiven herself. She teasingly quipped "I should have known that something fowl was afoot," as we all giggled and screamed with laughter rolling on the carpeted floor of our little sanctuary with great tears of joy running down our faces.

It was such an odd, yet joyous, experience that all this channeling and mediumship was unveiling. Soon after her revealing and healing, she returned to her celestial sanctuary. I could not imagine what was to come next.

Chapter 8

Sho Adh Shahanna Bhyong Mahadin

M y last employment in Tucson was with the Pima County jail, which became the Adult Detention Center of the Pima County Department of Corrections. This was a distinction that I was never able to fully appreciate. They couldn't fool me. I still knew that it was a jail. It was a dreary place, as most likely it should have been, though there had been substantial effort to make the new facility a little less dreary. Care was taken to ensure that every cell in the new jail would have a window to the outside world.

However, the employees had no windows. Though there was some relatively pleasing, infantry-blue and cream-colored paint splashed here and there, the new jail was still mostly concrete and steel. It felt like I was living in a bunker. Yes, there was the blessing of being able to go home every night and most weekends, but each workday I would have to return. True, the inmates pretty much had to stay there, twenty-four hours a day, seven days a week.

But as the years wore on, the realization slowly began to dawn on me that although the inmates would eventually leave, I was still there; and of my own volition!

Contrary to the outrageous constraints of political correctness, I have always identified with cowboys and see them as something special and worthy of admiration. Perhaps that is why I have sometimes been told that I have a bit of "shoot-from-the-hip" mentality. Part of my duties was to conduct an inmate orientation for those that the judge had decided would have to stay with us for awhile. I was rather fond of telling our new arrivals "to be careful, watch yourselves, because the people in here (jail) are insensitive, cruel and violent; then, of course, there are the inmates!"

Some just could not see past the tragedy of their own personal circumstances in order to appreciate my rather twisted sense of humor.

Some got it; some did not. I liked to pretend that, as a part of a comprehensive assessment for security level assignment, my wry remarks were probably not such a bad thing. By observing the inmates' reactions you could sometimes get an idea of their level of discomfort or emotional security. Looking back, it was probably the kind of humor that Hawk Woman would have enjoyed.

Some days my soul would ache to be able to spend some serious outside time—in nature, under the sun. I had spent weeks, months, and years feeling like I was living under the ground like a mole. Living with morally bankrupt, emotionally broken, and desperate people is not much fun. But somehow, I endured and prospered. I liked to think that I was able to bring something of goodness that might not have otherwise been there, had I not been present. But that is most likely a self-serving rationalization.

Now, I was sitting cross-legged beneath towering old-growth aspen. As gentle breezes swelled through the forest, leaves would rattle jubilantly leaving the impression of a great wistful sigh, casually cascading down the hillside and across a flower-studded meadow. Lunchtime gave me thirty minutes to reflect rather triumphantly; rejoicing in my good fortune, resting beneath the white-barked, green-topped forest.

Occasionally, I would be approached by a cautious cadre of feathered inquisitors who might be enticed to accept some morsel from my lunch box as an offering for my uninvited intrusion into their domain.

Across the canyon you could survey the many shades of emerald green on Sunshine Mesa and marvel at the beauty of snow-spattered granite that is Wilson Peak. Sometimes, with eyes closed, I would lie back in the tall grass, settling into the soft yielding earth and just listen to all the sounds: the running water in the stream, the prattling of birds, and the sound of my beating heart along with the subtle whisperings of an often elusive creator.

That summer, after finally finishing construction on the garage, I had secured a job as a general laborer and ductile pipe layer. I was in paradise. I was losing that paunch around my middle, and I didn't even have to diet or exercise. My body felt alive, powerful, and energized. This was welcomed, hard, physical work with the novel opportunity to be able to see that employment could actually lead to the creation of something worthwhile. I found it replete with a previously unknown sense of accomplishment. You knew you were providing people with something that they unquestionably needed. I was taking pride in knowing that what we were doing had lasting, palpable value. I was a part of efforts that would serve people for generations to come.

This was a treasured change after all the paper shuffling and endless hours of empty talking that too often riddled my "professional" experiences. That kind of work was like splashing vanishing footprints through a rushing stream. The construction work brought the clear satisfaction of knowing that deeply buried pipes would be bringing crystal-pure, life-sustaining, mountain water to untold thousands: feeding their lawns and gardens; gracing their kitchens; cleansing tired, aching bodies after hours of skiing; and quenching thirst generated by the thin, dry mountain air.

Okay, so I'm getting carried away, again. But at that time, that is the way it felt. That is the way I looked at it. That is the way it was.

It took awhile to be accepted. I had to downplay my education and previous professional positions. Folks couldn't understand why I took such a job. After all, I had a nice new house in Telluride,. and we were always taking "vacations," so I must be rich, right? Not the case.

We were comfortable, but not much more. Susan's transcribing began to suffer the ravages of being too far away from her clients. Finding employment in the general area of my expertise was either sporadic or nonexistent. There were a few months of savings left, but that was rapidly dwindling. Meanwhile, it was good to be allowed to do something that was healing to the mind, body, and soul. I had no doubt that eventually something more appropriate and financially sustaining would come along. But for the moment I was simply in paradise!

By late fall, the leaves had turned from yellow to gold and orange, and quickly began falling away. There had already been some substantial snow flurries in the town. In the high country, an encroaching crust of snow had begun creeping down the slopes, but not yet reaching into the valley. I reveled in the miracle of the low, dense clouds sporadically spewing forth an endless array of feathery white crystals, swirling and dancing in harmonious precision.

In the morning, the mud was usually frozen. Sometimes the job site looked like chocolate pudding sprinkled with powdered sugar. By mid-day as the ground began to melt, you could easily sink in up to your ankles. You had to be careful of the suction. It could pull rubber boots off your feet right in mid-stride. The black ooze was magnificent. I remembered all the time and effort we had put into composting the desert sand in a quest to enrich our garden back in Tucson. This soil was naturally rich, healthy; it was perfect.

There was still a lot of work to do, but some of us were getting laid off since the main facility of Telluride's new water treatment plant was mostly completed. Only one last stretch of the main line needed to be extended to connect with the valley floor. As I slid back down into the twelve-foot trench, the tamping machine began assaulting my ears again. The noise and gas fumes of the rattling gasoline engine gave me headaches. I was also becoming a little concerned about my hearing, having to say "What?" just a little too often. I remembered having a similar experience at a gunnery range in Fort Jackson, South Carolina. I was hopeful that this too would be temporary.

I had enjoyed the work immensely, but it was starting to wear on me. I had even been eyeing a Colorado real estate license; I considered becoming involved in one of Telluride's favorite burgeoning pasttimes—trading in condos. It was said that the economic base in Telluride was skiing, T-shirts, restaurants, lawyers that sued each other, and Realtors that sold each other real estate. Of course, the only real heroes were the contractors who built the stuff for all of us to enjoy and trade, within our little mountain playground.

Word came that the boss wanted to see me. Well, that was fine with me. There was a policy that first hired was last fired. It was probably my turn to go. To my surprise, I had been selected to go to Cortez, a town about seventy miles to the south. It seems that they had run out of tires for one of their pieces of heavy equipment. They needed either repairs or replacements. Since I had absolutely no experience in fitting heavy equipment with huge tires, I was naturally chosen. It was a welcomed respite from my sentencing to the trench. It was becoming a bit too wet, too cold, and monotonous. And, I had to admit it, at times my paradise was becoming just a tad dreary.

As I returned home the sun was setting. It was already casting a cold, darkening shadow across the valley. A layer of lazy gray smoke hung a few hundred feet above the town. You could see the little dots of lights in the houses and the last shades of a pink sunset on the snow-spattered peaks, glowing just above the high alpine basins. Ben came out all excited and gazed incredulously at the giant tires on the back of the flatbed truck.

The kids had already eaten. I pulled off muddy clothes, shook them, and tossed them at the washing machine. While Susan busied herself in the kitchen, I stumbled into the bathroom and collapsed into the shower, languishing in the tub awhile and praising whatever god that there might be for inventing hot water.

As I lay there, suspended in thought, I heard the faint sound of a giggling child. Then there was a knock on the door. I presumed the kids were looking for me. But, when I looked, no one was there. As I dried off and put on my evening lounging clothes, all I could hear was a droning television in the background.

Susan wrapped her arms around me, clinging tightly for an especially long hug. I ambled over to the kitchen counter, straddled a stool, and began to eat. After the usual chitchat and other pleasantries, Susan retired to the office and resumed typing. Downstairs, I remember hearing Ben and Jessica battling over the piano, while Mollie attempted an unsuccessful mediation.

Again, I heard child-like giggling. I got up and looked around but Susan was the only one who was there. It was probably the television. So, I sauntered over to the refrigerator and opened it looking for a final course to supplement my evening feast. As I turned to close the door, she was peering around the corner. She giggled and then ducked behind the door jamb and disappeared into the next room. A moment later she was peaking at me again.

Then, Susan explained, "I think there is someone here who wants to meet you."

Timidly, with a gaze of playful dancing eyes of considerable affection, she started speaking words that seemed oddly familiar, but my mind could not quite comprehend. There was a smattering of hard consonants, long vowels, an occasional click, and an abundance of "atl" sounds. Then, she briefly transitioned into a dialect of English that was barely comprehensible, a sort of contorted baby talk.

Susan was at it again. This time, it was a delightful little child. She had been timidly playing hide-and-seek with me. She looked around the house a moment with wide eyes that contained all the excitement that you might expect to see on a child's face on Christmas morning. She moved across the floor in tiny little steps with a gait that was not unsteady, but perhaps a little rushed and clumsy. She would rather coyly shrug her shoulders as she locked her elbows and clumsily wrung her hands, turning her head to one side with a sort of sheepish grin. She presented in much the same manner as a precocious five-year-old girl.

What could I do? I watched and wondered, attempted to communicate. But, every time I would start to talk she would just look at me and giggle. After a very short time she wandered back into the home office located just off the kitchen. Susan re-emerged and seemed curious about the odd expression that was on my face. Then she went back to her typing, saying she had to get her work out because the Source wanted to talk to us later on in the evening.

Later, it was explained that this "little one" was a past life of Susan, and that she was being placed into "your capable hands" in order for us to learn about that lifetime and to grow into the benefits that the experience would ultimately bring. The Source indicated that, although some might tend to consider this to be a psychological disorder, this was not so.

This was supposedly "a method of bringing together aspects of an individual soul from several lifetimes into one, which would result in much healing and benefit for the entity" (Susan).

During the next few weeks there were a number of episodes in which this little one appeared. She slowly became more accustomed to her surroundings as she explored, prodded, and observed. Susan mostly knew when she was around, but not always. The channel indicated that it was a lot like when the Source was coming through. She could hear and was aware of what was going on, but things seemed to transpire rather involuntarily.

As things progressed, Susan could easily interrupt the process somewhat at will, adding her own observations and questions with the Source generally responding out loud, so that I could follow this unfettered eruption of her internal dialogue. Susan could usually interact with the little one if they were both present. Sometimes the child would be very energetic and active, while Susan might be tired. Sometimes the child would be tired and sleep with Susan being very active and alert. The channel would direct and comfort the child as a sort of surrogate parent-child relationship evolved.

I eventually became known as "Tati" while Susan became known as "Mati Susan." This was how we were introduced to the one we came to know as Sho Adh Shannah Bhyong Mahadin. She simply refered to herself as "Sha Sha," since she was too young to pronounce her full name without considerable assistance from the Source.

We would not hear from this little one for days at a time. Then, she would be around; in and out as it were, for hours. It took her awhile to acclimate, but it didn't take as long as Hawk Woman. Never did she seem to be intrusive. Our daily schedules and family activities were almost never impeded or disrupted. When an interruption did occur, it was a brief and relatively minor occurrence.

We developed a habit of playing some music at night as we were drifting off to sleep. Sha Sha, if present, would sometimes sing along. I awoke one night to hear Susan singing in a child-like voice. For well over an hour, Sha Sha would sing advertising jingles. There may have been a couple of dozen of them. Most of them came from the era when Susan and I were growing up. It was incredible. Musical jingles and slogans that we had not heard for decades were coming to the forefront: Oscar Mayer wieners, Bumble Bee tuna, Ipana toothpaste, Hamm's beer, Pall Mall cigarettes, seeing the USA in your Chevrolet, just to name a few.

Intermittently, Susan would laugh and we would reminisce, remembering all the catchy little tunes and slogans that were woven into our childhood. After awhile, Susan would interrupt and say "Okay, Sha Sha, it is time for sleep now. No more singing."

We would fall back to sleep and before long Sha Sha would be at it again. The child explained that the Source was helping her look at Mati Susan's mind and that she was finding all these "funny little things" inside of it.

The Source explained that this was an exercise that was helping the child to become more familiar with the culture and language and make it easier for her to participate in the present lifetime. It seems that Susan's basic fund of knowledge and abilities were being steadily accessed by her young visitor.

The child once asked where Baby Susan was. She inquired because apparently Sha Sha had occasionally been allowed to play with Susan when she was a toddler. It took a long time for Sha Sha to grasp the notion that Susan was now the grown woman of the child that Sha Sha at one time had visited. She told a story of how she watched Mati Susan fly through a window when she was born.

One morning, when Susan had been in the bathroom, Sha Sha came running into the kitchen full of tears and screaming.

"Tati! Tati! There's an ugly old woman in the bathroom!"

Sha Sha seemed more surprised and confused than frightened. So, I encouraged her to go back so we could take a look. No one was there. Later in the day, we figured it out; the child had seen Susan's image in the mirror and was unnerved by it. When Susan realized that it was her own face in the mirror that Sha Sha had seen (the ugly old woman), Susan chuckled rather stoically and wryly responded,

"Thanks a lot, Sha Sha!"

At first it was very hard for Sha Sha to comprehend that she was visiting us by inhabiting Susan's body. Later she came to look at this as if she and Susan would sometimes share the same body or "dolly" as she liked to call the physical body.

Sometimes Sha Sha didn't like the way Susan was combing "her" hair. Sha Sha thought Susan was being too rough and taking too long. Sha Sha once recognized the traditional ceremonial hairstyles of Hopi Indian women and emphatically held to the belief that this was how her hair was to look. There will be more discussion on this later.

For those who have not had the opportunity to observe such a transformation, these descriptions may seem a bit hard to believe. If I had not witnessed and intimately lived and interacted with all that was Susan on a daily basis, I too might question the authenticity and legitimacy of such claims. I assure the reader that every word is essentially true. There may be slight unintended distortions or the fading of memories here or there, but this was as real as anything I have ever experienced.

There were some rather interesting aspects of this phenomenon. While Sha Sha could sing very well, with perfect pitch, Susan had never been able to find or stay on key when singing. Susan was left-handed. Sha Sha was right-handed. They had a preference for different kinds of foods. Facial expressions and mannerisms were completely different when the child was present.

Remember, this author was one who was professionally trained, skilled, and experienced in the nature of the human psyche and behavior. Many years were spent working with acute, chronic, mental health patients; witnessing and assessing aberrations and maladies of all kinds, including folks who were under the influence of mind-altering chemical substances.

When I was employed at Kino Community Hospital in Tucson, I encountered several patients with a diagnosis of dissociative identity disorder, which is more commonly known as a multiple personality disorder. There had even been opportunities to participate in the treatment of persons deemed to have multiple personalities; but none of them came close to what was being witnessed in my own home on a daily basis. Never have I experienced anything like what was going on with Susan; before or since.

Multiple personalities generally come to the attention of mental health professionals due to health and safety concerns. Most often, the emergence of these personalities is exceedingly disruptive and maladaptive to the overall functioning of the client.

In all cases in which I was associated, the individuals had angry, hostile, maladaptive aspects of an original personality that had become fractured. They were often at war with one another.

I have seen madness up close—real close. The voices of psychotic patients are predominately obsessive, repetitive, and destructive. Actual conversation is very limited. The patients are mostly too disorganized or distracted to effectively communicate anything of significant value. And, there is little that might be considered to be teachings or meaningful, coherent discourse. Those clinical presentations were not even close to being as comprehensive and detailed as were the personalities that were being exhibited through Susan.

In assessing mental illness, mental health professionals often use a qualifying differential. Paraphrasing, it goes something like this:

> If an individual has not demonstrated a present danger to self
> or others either by history or current circumstance; and if the in-
> dividual can carry on all the normal functions required for daily
> living, then a diagnosis of mental illness is suspect.

One of my mentors, a very successful, teaching psychiatrist, was fond of saying that there were all kinds of people doing and believing all kinds of things out there. Over and over again, he would remind us that in the future, the way we diagnose and treat mental disturbances (during the seventies and eighties) will be seen as crude and as ignorant as the way that mental health patients were treated during the Dark Ages.

Always did he suggest that the first question we must ask of ourselves, and of our patient, is whether or not the presenting condition is a problem or not; whether it essentially interferes with the functioning of the individual to provide for their liveli-hood as well as health and safety needs or general quality of life. If not, then we were entreated to question whether or not it was a condition that required significant intervention or treatment.

Over time things do change. I once witnessed a client receiv-ing a dissociative identity disorder diagnosis simply because some days she dressed in a suit as a business woman, and an-other times she enjoyed feeling like a "free spirit," dressing like a hippie with loose fitting, brightly colored clothes. Of course, to-day, the state of the "helping professions" has deteriorated to the point that, in some circles, one's mental health can be ques-tioned by a licensed practicioner merely because there is a disagreement over political issues.

Nevertheless, a part of me always kept a critical clinical eye toward these goings on; both within the family and within the psyche of my beloved.

At times there were doubts and soul searching for us both. But never could we come to the conclusion that this was other than what this Source had suggested: a looking back into differ-ent incarnations of the soul.

This is a level of confidence that could only come through years of living day to day with the channel, through both rewarding and difficult times. Whatever was going on here, there was much more depth and intensity than what the vast majority of the mental health community can imagine, unless they have personally been through it themselves.

The current response to these conditions seems to rather impotently fall into a few limited approaches. One is to ignore the behavior, assuming it will go away if it is not reinforced because it is simply maladaptive learned behavior.

Another is to treat, with drugs, any abnormalities that the individuals might exhibit. For example if one personality is depressed you give the body antidepressants, whether or not anyone else is depressed.

The third is to simply act as if it is true, in a nonjudgmental manner and accept the personalities and respond to them accordingly. If the particular personality appears to be a child, then you treat them as a child and raise them. The endgame is to get them all happy and comfortable and become integrated again. But I get the sense that the process is one in which the therapist mostly observes and supports rather than intervenes or orchestrates. And, this was my wife; not a patient.

If not welcome, a multiple personality tends not to publicly emerge unless under substantial stress. They will tend not to emerge unless they feel safe, supported, and unjudged. If you ignore them or dismiss them, they really do not go away. They just get quiet, watch, and wait, emerging at another time within more accepting circumstances. Therapists with a behavioral approach either do not know this, or they simply do not care. The condition can't be dealt with by their paradigm.

It was our conclusion that this process with Susan was no simple identity disorder or psychosis, but a deep adventure into the soul of humankind from beyond our ignorant and limited ways of current acceptance and understanding.

This was a quantum leap into mostly unexplored states of consciousness. And, there are many thousands of Susans out there. There is a whole harvest of souls opening up and blooming right before us, if we could but recognize and comprehend this miraculous process.

Susan, with her particular condition, seemed to be as coherent, orderly, and under control as any other "normal" person. She was able to take care of her children and to work and go about all the activities of a person in what we would term a normal state of consciousness.

She was not a danger to herself or others. Except for a few fleeting moments, she seldom doubted or considered herself to be anything other than a psychic channel who was living in the midst of other lifetimes in which she would sometimes move back and forth through different ages and dimensions.

Sha Sha would sometimes feel a little competitive. The Source was capable of talking through Sha Sha as well as Susan. Hawk Woman, once acclimated, seemed to be of a more pure, direct, and personal connection. At times, when Susan was tired or otherwise distressed, the Source seemed to prefer speaking through Sha Sha. Supposedly, this surrogate channeling was also helpful in keeping the contacts and interactions between the aspects of the entity clearer and more balanced, thereby creating an ongoing transitioning process that would be easier and more complete.

At one point, it seems that Hawk Woman had been looking into the mind of the child, Sha Sha, while the "Feathered Presence" was honing her contemporary language skills. So for a brief time, the old bird began talking the "baby talk" that she had gleaned from the little one. When she finally figured out why she sounded so odd and how this had happened, she was highly incensed. She felt she had been somehow tricked into talking the baby talk and made to look ridiculous.

Later we teased her, saying that she really got her feathers ruffled. Eventually she was able to see the humor in it and even pretended to talk like the "Pussycat," which was a reference to my alleged guardian spirit, the jaguar.

One day, the child became quite restless and was tired of having the Source speak through her for readings. She interrupted the process and stated rather defiantly:

"I am tired of all this babbling. It's silly"

She giggled a bit and erupted again. "Blah! Blah! Blah!"

She started flopping her mouth up and down saying that the Source made her do it and she couldn't talk and say what she wanted to say. So the little one started calling the Source, "Babbling."

The Source responded, saying that she was a child and not intending to be disrespectful. It was explained that it was sometimes hard for her to sit still and be controlled by "the energies." (However, I did observe that on occasion she would be taken away, back into Susan's psche, if the child became a little too unruly.)

It was given that the child could use the name "Babbling" for the Source without criticism or reservation. It seemed to have stuck. And, every so often you could hear her lilting little voice beginning with "Babbling say ..."

Most often, Susan would then come to the forefront and finish whatever there was to be imparted or made available to those present. After a few years, she could speak the words of her Source in a crowd or during a public dinner conversation with none but the family or our most intimate friends knowing what was transpiring.

In time, Sha Sha learned to impersonate Susan. So Sha Sha "a la" Susan could go out into the community and experience what the culture had to offer, and learn, and grow. She would sometimes become so good at it that not even I would notice. Usually, it would start by Susan saying some very odd or ignorant sounding things that I would find annoying.

She would start asking a myriad of mundane questions, or make some rather odd observations or assumptions until I suddenly realized that it was not Susan, but Sha Sha using Susan's voice and mannerisms. What might be annoying for an adult to say made perfect sense for a child, especially a child from a different time and culture.

I would inquire, "Sha Sha, is that you?"

And from out of Susan's mature, centered countenance would emerge a happy, smiling little face with a short giggle. "Yes, Tati it's me."

Again, the Source always seemed to be there as a step-by-step process to guide, direct, suspend, and protect, so that none would be unduly harmed. However, the process of going through the experience was at times quite stressful as our understanding and concept of reality evolved. Our worldview was greatly tested and expanded.

Eventually, much of the communication from the Source tended to be in the form of words that were heard "in her head" and passed on by the channel; thus making her more of a reporter of the information rather than appearing as a "puppet of the forces." This form of channeling was seen as a more complete and advanced method, for "one did not have to go to sleep or be in trance to hear or express the words of God."

The Source often reiterated that "for these purposes" had Susan and I been brought together. And "for these purposes" the child had been delivered into my "capable hands."

And, that as we would choose, so would the journey would continue ...

Chapter 9

Mokhi Maya

Susan once traveled through Mexico, deep into the heart of the Yucatan peninsula. Even as a child, she had a strong interest in the history and culture of Meso America. According to her story, she was twenty-three years old when she and her friend, Jane, decided to escape from New York City and go exploring.

They had both been intermittently active in off-Broadway theatre productions and gotten to know each other quite well while working on a number of creative projects. Susan was in costuming and Jane was a sculptor. Jane was often called upon to create unusual pieces that were used on stage and even in movies. Her main claim to fame was her creation of a variety of huge ceramic penises for the movie called, *A Clockwork Orange*. In one defining home-invasion scene, the main characters were ransacking a home that sported a rather odd taste in art. During an orgy of vandalism, Jane's masterpiece was summarily shattered, thus providing the shocking effect that the director had envisioned.

The girls flew to Mexico City and rented a car. Jane did all the chauffeuring since Susan had not yet learned to drive. She had been stranded in New York City her whole life, where handling an automobile was not an essential skill. The young explorers traversed through mountains, deserts, savannas, and tropical rainforests, taking in many sights. Susan in particular became enchanted with the many ancient ruins they began to encounter. Traveling deep into the Mexican jungle, they even hired a guide in order to locate and visit several remote sites.

Eventually the girls abandoned their vehicle and caught a plane that could get them into Guatemala. It was described as an old DC-3, a World War II troop and cargo carrier. The plane had been used to transport a load of tomatoes just prior to their boarding. Apparently, quite a number of tomatoes were left on the plane, rotting in the oppressive heat of the Yucatan. Metal seats were mounted along the walls inside the fuselage where passengers could sit. When not in use, the seats could be folded up against the side of the plane in order to reconfigure space so that cargo could be more easily accommodated.

I remember tales of loose, rattling rivets slowly turning around in the plane's exposed superstructure, while sputtering engines propelled them through emerald mountain passes. Susan also described a number of oddly-spaced holes in the plane's side, large enough to poke their fingers through.

They arrived in Guatemala and walked right into a local military coup. The area was overrun by soldiers carrying automatic weapons who were in the process of securing the airport. The craft slowly lumbered just above the top of trees, clipping a few branches in its final approach, and stopping just before the dirt runway ended.

Susan would explain that it looked more like a simple landing strip where supplies were delivered rather than an actual airport. Would-be passengers, with grim expressions languished behind gated fences while being searched and questioned.

As Susan related the story, the officials posted at the airport were rather surprised that the girls had not heard what was happening. Apparently, there was amazement and shock that they were even able to get into Guatemala at that particular time and location. Susan had spent a summer as an intern in a Latin American embassy in New York, so her Spanish was adequate; but it sometimes took some doing to find the right words to communicate. Jane was portrayed a monolingual wallflower and had little idea of what was going on without Susan's labored translations.

It was a dangerous situation. They were in a culture where proper young ladies did not travel alone. And they were in the middle of a military coup with a potential for full insurrection. Several times gunfire erupted in the distance. Along one side of the clearing were several thatched huts with matted floors that travelers were allowed to use as overnight shelter. I can imagine how alien and terrifying the scene must have been for two girls who grew up in the canyons of New York, City.

Apparently, providence came to the rescue. The next day a distinguished-looking, well-dressed, Hispanic gentleman showed up with three sons who had heard of the plight of the two young ladies from America. He was described as a person of some importance. Susan said the soldiers kept their distance as they smiled and nodded, taking direction from him.

Soon, the girls were assigned an armed guide and were off, down the road again to explore more ruins. Although I have forgotten a lot of the details of her adventure, it does appear that they eventually got back home safely and supposedly were none the worse for wear.

When Susan was a child, she recalled having dreams and even visions of huge temples and colorfully dressed people who were mostly just involved in everyday activities. At other times, she witnessed epic celebrations with dancing, singing, and the beating of huge drums.

Mollie, Susan's mother, used to tell us that when Suzy was a toddler, just barely able to talk, she would tell anyone who would listen that at night she would fly out the window. She told stories of visiting her other family, and that there was a "big lady" who would always show her the way back home.

Upstairs, in an old armoire, along with the recorded readings and other keepsakes, is a marvelous necklace. It was given to my beloved as she was returning from her visit to Tikal, an ancient Mayan city. She said that an old man with deep, penetrating blue eyes and weathered hands came out of a crowd of street vendors and placed it around her neck. He told her that she was a priestess and he had been waiting for her to return.

A moment later he disappeared back into the crowd. The eyes were very familiar; she had seen them in her dreams many times. However, after his presentation, she was unable to find him and never dreamed of him again. The Source claimed it was an angel.

The necklace is rather magnificent. It is made from finely-crafted, heavy silver with a Mayan-looking head carved out of lapis. On rare occasions, Susan would carefully clean and slowly drape the talisman around her neck. It was usually a time when there was some kind of transition or change coming into our lives.

The object has a very curious habit of disappearing. It will be missing for months or even years at a time. Then one day you will find it again, right where it was supposed to be, but apparently not where you could always find it. Sometimes, if you hold it awhile, sitting in meditation, you can see glimpses of other times and places. It is a thing that can help you remember.

Right about the time of the emergence of Hawk Woman, the Source had commented that, yes indeed, Susan had been a priestess in an ancient culture that had once blossomed in a region we now call the Yucatan. From time to time, the little one would make mention of it, telling us stories about her home where she lives when she is not with her Tati and Mati Susan.

Here and there, Susan would have glimpses of this distant and vaguely familiar place; somewhere back in time. She was never sure if these were Sha Sha's images or of her own remembering. The Source, through the years, would offer and confirm bits and pieces of information as our own personal life story unfolded within this current time and culture. Eventually, by these means and others, it became possible to put together a general picture or description of a place that supposedly existed well before what we now call recorded history.

Around fifteen to twenty-five thousand years ago immigrants were still fleeing from the last vestiges of the Atlantean continent as it subsided into what is now known as the Atlantic Ocean. Several groups of people began a migration into the Yucatan in what we now call Central America, giving birth to a fledgling colony: first just to survive, then to create a new culture, hoping to remember the tragic lessons of the previous generations. Some of these peoples were supposedly from a root race of an evolving ethnicity that much, much later became known as the Mayan civilization.

According to the Source, modern archaeologists as well as other scientists have not yet discovered just how ancient these cultures are. The Source would tell us that mankind's sojourn on Earth should be measured in hundreds of thousands of years, not merely in tens of thousands of years. These teachings have indicated that it is not uncommon for certain regions to be reinhabited over and over again with several related cultures emerging, declining to extinction, and then emerging once again. People who originally inhabited these sanctuaries will often return, in another lifetime, after many millenniums with memories embedded deeply in their souls; stirred by incomplete longings for unfulfilled glories, which they yet hope to attain or to simply reaffirm.

We were told that the ancient culture in question was founded around a great teacher who in modern parlance would best be described as a priestess. This was a time in which the direct connection that most had enjoyed with what we call the Source had diminished considerably. So, in this and many subsequent cultures, it was not uncommon for people to form around one whose connection was still clear and strong—rich in wisdom and divine purpose. Through this Priestess, which today we might also refer to as an oracle or channel, information was offered to help guide the populace through the difficult times of forming a newer version of an evolving colony from the previous, Andaluvian empire.

Eventually, a sort of theocratic dynasty evolved. These were not leaders who ruled so much by despotic coercion, but rather led through inspiration and trust earned by means of the quality and usefulness of the wisdom that was offered—both through and from those inspired channels.

During each generation, a soul would be born into the culture that would be appointed through a channel of the Source, and affirmed by the people, as being the new High Priest or Priestess that would continue to guide the fledgling civilization. This process is somewhat similar to what was utilized in the Tibetan culture in which there is one known as the Dalai Lama. Thus, as the generations continued, the Source would anoint a progression of individuals who would serve as the primary spiritual leader through each of the succeeding generations.

However, in the culture now being described, there would be a different soul selected for each generation; not a reincarnation of the same soul over and over again. Supposedly, something in the divine nature of the universe would select a soul that had both the capacity and necessary associations in previous lives to become the next spiritual leader.

There was a cadre of others who would also manifest a variety of intuitive gifts. These others were sometimes referred to by the Source as a sort of priest clan. All were encouraged to pray, meditate, celebrate, and establish their own relationship with their creator. However, for cultural and social purposes, there was only one appointed High Priest or Priestess.

This leader was not seen so much as a perfect being, but rather one chosen and imbued with gifts and skills apropos to the time and place in order to continue to offer guidance from the vast heavenly realms of spirit from which we have all supposedly sprung. The acceptance of the authenticity and divinity of the Priest Clan, as well as trust in the forces that emanated through them, was the cohesive foundation that kept the culture unified, working in harmony, and progressing.

Both a priest clan faction and a sort of administrative faction evolved within this culture. Although the Priest Clan did not rule by dictatorial authority, it was difficult to say no or to ignore suggestions, since it was the general belief and understanding that the gods themselves were directing the decisions and activities of the chosen spiritual leader. So obviously, the High Priest or Priestess would often be the most influential leader in the culture. This archetypical pattern can also be observed and recognized right into some of our contemporary cultures and institutions. It should be strongly emphasized that this was not the modern Mayan culture that had fallen into superstition, blood sacrifice, and endless warfare. This was supposedly an ancient and golden age that flourished thousands of years before the modern Mayans.

As described, this was a marvelous time, a new beginning for a new civilization in which anything was possible. Imagine an entire culture where the people had the capacity, for better or for worse, to believe and accept that God had appointed a guide, a priestly messenger to speak a divine message and to offer a blue-print for the future, and to offer sacred ways to handle distress and contention.

That doesn't happen very often. When is does, it is usually short-lived since the authenticity and worthiness of the leaders tends to devolve into a sort of narcissistic arrogance, which can result in an abuse of their power, along with a rather unattractive exaggerated view of their own personal importance. Thus, the people can become harnessed to earthly masters: enslaved through earthly coercion, rather than being empowered, inspired, and free to creatively celebrate all that life has to offer.

When that happens, the divine forces usually withdraw or, perhaps better stated, are abandoned and become wizened. Meanwhile, the impotent and often corrupt, hollow vessels remain, but are devoid of significant light, wisdom, or insight. Then, so it would seem, the Source goes hunting elsewhere, to a place where the soil might be fertile, where the gifts might once again be awakened and valued.

The Source explained that, after approximately three hundred years of immigration and growth, this tribal kingdom within the heart of the Yucatan, had a population of over one-hundred-thousand. At that time, there were other forming and evolving cultures in the same region from which trade and similar teachings were interspersed.

All this transpired over several generations during which upheavals in Earth's climate and geography forced relocation from once safe and productive regions to new locations where humankind might first survive and then flourish once more.

The coastal areas in the Yucatan were farther inland than what is seen today. Much of this is due to the shifting and reshuffling of the earth's massive tectonic plates, after the catastrophic shifting of the poles and displacement of the polar ice caps. There was also the influence of fluctuations of solar activity that sometimes induces a series of ice ages, which are predicted to come again. The general atmosphere and climate at that time was described as being similar to what it is now, but a bit more moderate.

Temple cities and administrative centers were usually built of stone. These were often pyramid shaped, but there were also other geometric forms. These buildings were covered with brightly colored stuccos, frescos and even tapestries, depending on their level of importance to the culture's evolving heritage.

Generally, there was an attempt to place buildings in such a manner that they would mimic constellations in the heavens. Sometimes, the placement of several hamlets within a particular region would also be configured upon a particular stellar constellation. This, of course, would also depend upon the natural geographic features of the land and the subsequent suitability for habitation and commerce.

At the center of the culture was a temple city where the leaders of the Priest Clan resided. From there, a loosely knit series of communities were scattered about, each with its own sanctified sites and even individualized customs that formed a part of the pantheon of the society as a whole.

An administrative arm was developed in order to carry out the organizational requirements of the society. It was the custom for the Priestess to offer appointments to these few and flexible, positions that tended to the day-to-day needs of the people.

In concert with the priestly functions, the administrative arm served more like a cadre of coordinators and consultants rather than a rigid bureaucracy. However, it was also their prerogative to provide mediation whose judgments, if necessary, could be backed by a sort of royal guard of constables who were highly trained in what could be termed the martial arts.

These militant or constabulatory functions were mostly based upon a sense of loyalty and commitment to the patrons

and the traditions of the offices which they would serve and protect. These *guards* could also be called upon to defend unwel-
come intrusions in the borderlands, as well as to quell out of
control internal feuds that might lead to insurrection. However, I
am left with the impression that these struggles were few and
short-lived.

The culture was based on what might best be termed a clan
system of interlocking professions and functions; each clan tending to reside in a particular locality, but not exclusively. Each
tended to embody a particular responsibility, seen as a coveted
opportunity to contribute to the whole.

The mind-set seemed to be one of having great pride in being
able to offer up to the community their particular services,
goods, or expertise. There were those who provided agricultural
products; those who were skilled in building or as artisans or
healers; those who defended and adjudicated conflict, though
much of that was left up to the wisdom of the local priesthood
which was appointed by the high priest or priestess; all supposedly functioning under the influence of divine forces.

Several times a year the people would come together around
the temple city and celebrate through great pageantry, dancing,
singing, and storytelling. They would both remember and be
taught by the Priest Clan through the High Priestess; and by the
Source, that which would lead them in the ways of peace, pros-
perity, and spiritual enlightenment.

Early on, the Source had explained to us that this little Sha Sha
had been chosen to be a Priestess as a vessel of the procession of
universal spirit as made manifest to these people of the Yucatan.

As was the custom, the Source would quicken the spirit of
the reigning priest(ess) so that the child could be found and identified. Then, the High Priestess while still living, would issue a
public proclamation that the child had been found. Eventually,
arrangements would be made to provide the guidance and training for this child who would become the next High Priest or

Priestess. Thus would the words, the knowledge, the encouragement, and the wisdom of the Source be made available to guide
the people for the succeeding generation.

And, of course, it was our understanding that this little one
who called herself Sha Sha, was Susan in that previous lifetime.

The Hopi Indians of the Four Corners area of the south-
western United States have some very ancient practices and
teachings. One precept is the belief that there were migrations in
the four directions from an original center of the earth. Through
the millennia, the generations would travel the face of the western world; north, south, east, and west, including Central America, and perhaps beyond. Thus would be left behind remnants of
this original people, along with their teachings and culture, in
many places across the globe. Some even believe there are
ancient connections as far west as Jerusalem.

If I understand correctly, some of these remnants eventually
returned to the center in the Southwest, both reviving and continuing their cultural traditions. Some teachings assert that a
core of Hopi people have lived and reincarnated within these
original sanctuaries since the beginnings of mankind's infusion
into the planet. Their task is to remember and to keep the sacred
knowledge alive—offering up ceremonies, teachings, and prophecy when directed to do so.

When at the Source's insistence, Susan and I gained entrance
to Orabi, in Hopi Land, little Sha Sha became very excited and
enamored of these native people. She strongly identified with
them and told us that they were a part of her people. She delighted in learning that they shared a number of similar spiritual
practices and beliefs. She told us how her teacher would put her
hair up in the same butterfly style that the Hopi women still use
on special ceremonial occasions.

She remembered them from her home in the Yucatan, as well as from her visitations to our time and place. Though patient and respectful, she was always resolute on these issues of who she was and where she came from. She would not be dissuaded.

She did this because her clan was supposedly seeded from these Hopi people who had migrated and eventualy became the formal leadership of her culture.

The more original pronunciation and consequent spelling of these indigenous people is closer to Mokhi, rather than Hopi.

Again, this period that the Source was referring to in which the child priestess lived, came into being many thousands of years before the more recent Mayan civilization of the Yucatan that our modern scientists and historians are currently exploring.

Due to her obvious attachment to the Hopis, the little one rather recalcitrantly dubbed her homeland "Mokhi Maya" a term which the Source supported as, "... being reasonably accurate for the purposes of the entity."

And who were we to quibble with one born to become the High Priestess of "Mokhi Maya"?

Fort Hood Texas

Five-year-old Sha Sha with her Priestess Necklace

The necklace from Guatemala

"Mati Susan"

Sha Sha's present to Tati—
"So you won't forget me."

"Tati"

Mayan ruins from Susan's travels

Susan on pilgrimage—remembering

"The Mountain" Telluride, Colorado

Telluride home

Susan in Tucson

Susan with children

Susan receiving communication from Source

Being silly

"Hawk Woman"

"Baby Self" communing with Hawk Mother (Mother Mary)

"The channel who speaks and
the channel who does not speak"

Susan 24 hours before transition

Family memorial to Susan

Chapter 10

A Precious Treasure: The Duality Unravels

It has been said that where there is the potential for great good, there is also the potential for great evil.

Earlier in the day I had chased down the Federal Express truck that I caught meandering down Main Street. After a couple of brutal days in front of the computer, without much sleep, Susan had come through once again. It was a long tedious transcript. In Tucson, court dates had been set and there were appeals to be addressed. Though sprung upon her at the last minute, another important "due date" had been met.

But, Susan had been increasingly troubled and distracted. She was going through the motions, but she didn't quite seem to be involved in her environment. There had been little contact with the Source. When it did manifest, it seemed short and had a bit of a somber tone. Sha Sha was not around much. When she did emerge she seemed to be regressing. A couple of times I caught her asleep, sucking her thumb and clutching a small stuffed pony. She said she liked the little pony because it only ate stardust and never needed a diaper.

It was one of those late evenings when the moon was full. Susan had showered and towel dried her waist-length hair, which was still damp. She began combing it out strand by strand as she stared out the second story window of our cramped, loft-shaped bedroom. I have always been enamored of women with long hair. I know it requires a lot of time and care. I often wondered if she kept it that way just to please me. But, then again, her hair had always been long. Sha Sha insisted it be that way so she could put it up in butterfly fashion like the Hopi women used to do.

We had turned the bed around so that the head was facing north. I sat on the bed behind her, helping with some of the tangles that were particularly troublesome. A couple of times the little one surfaced. She was irritable and cranky. She didn't like having her hair pulled. She was untrusting and seemed a little frightened. I gently massaged her shoulders, back, and legs. It was one of those times when I wasn't really sure who I was massaging. Susan and her minions collapsed into the soft feather bed, relaxing into a deep and well-deserved sleep. I pulled the covers up around her as she murmured and clutched her pillow.

I heard a soft little voice say "Thank you, Tati."

I gently closed the door to our bedroom and crossed the narrow landing and entered the twilight of our meditation room. It was a time when the east side of town was a lot less developed. Because of the fullness of the moon you could see through the darkness, up into the outline of the massive granite peaks that dwarf the little town. It was a night full of the images of shadow-casting trees and rocks that glistened with fresh forming dew.

I always found the cool moist air to be quite refreshing. If the window had been opened, I might have taken a few moments to listen to the crisp rush and rattle of the San Miguel River, a mere hundred yards away. I might have even nudged the crystal that hung in the window absorbing the primal power of the sacred

mountain. It might have been one of those times when I wondered if the crystal might be capable of refracting a little moonlight across the shadowed, gray walls; perhaps that was just a
fanciful illusion.

Sensing something ominous, I sat upon my sheepskin rug
and assumed a comfortable yogic posture and prepared for meditation. As was my custom at the time, I most likely engaged in a
little pranayamic breathing. I remember that the meditation
didn't seem to do much to dispel what I was feeling. It was one of
those highly tactile, unsettling times that just kept becoming
more and more intense. Soon, I too fell asleep.

I awoke with Winchester, the family dog, sniffing at my face.
He was sometimes quite confounded by bouts of snoring. Perhaps he had come to investigate. Still half asleep, I clumsily lumbered back across the darkened hall, trying not to trip over my
inquisitive four-footed companion, and quickly slid into bed. I
reached out to Susan but she was not there, no doubt she was
downstairs in the bathroom or perhaps checking on the kids.

Then, as if climbing out of a dream, I thought I heard something. I sat up, but there was nothing there. I lay back down for a
moment. Then, there it was again. But, what was it? I heard it
again; a sort of muffled whimper. I got up and looked around. Susan was nowhere to be found. Once again all was quiet. I called
out to her.

Through the shadowed darkness I heard someone sobbing.
My fingers timidly searched for the tiny switch on the petite,
stained-glass lamp that was somewhere in the niche of the head-
board. The little bulb came to life. The dimly lit room was quiet
and empty. Susan was nowhere to be found. Then, I thought I
heard a rustling sound from behind the little door that lead to the
storage compartment behind the wall. Crawling on my knees, I
reached for the knob and called her name. The door flew open.

She immediately lunged, desperately clinging to me like a
flailing rock climber dangling from the face of a cliff. She sobbed

and squealed, shaking uncontrollably, almost looking as if she were going into convulsions.

In an attempt to stifle her wailing, she pulled her nightgown over her head and tightly clamped her hands over her mouth. She almost began to suffocate. Then she would take huge desperate breaths and begin screaming in great terror with clenched words that were impossible to understand.

I held her tightly and encouraged her to take slow, deep breaths. She was perspiring profusely and her heart was pounding so hard I could feel it right through her chest. Pulling at me she almost dragged me through the door and into little closet. With shaking hands she quickly slammed the door with a force strong enough to loosen some of the molding. As we lay in the darkness she sobbed over and over "It's Mati! It's Mati! Don't let her hurt us!"

I tried to comfort her and told her that she was just having a bad dream. She started to breathe more normally and began speaking in a loud, raspy whisper. I told her she was safe and I would not let anyone hurt her. Her vice-grip on my arm began to relax. Against her protests, I eventually coaxed open the door to show her that no one was there to hurt us. We crawled out of the closet and I turned up the lights and got her to sit up. With much trepidation, I convinced her to walk around the room and to peer into the hall and down the lighted stairway. We went back to bed and the little one once again fell asleep in my arms.

A little later, Susan sat up looking pale, haggard, and exhausted. She looked at me with that thousand-yard stare and said something like, "Well, that was quite a night. I wonder what's going to happen next." Then she too laid the body back down and both mother and child were fast asleep. She had been like a spectator during the entire incident but was unable to suppress the little one and regain control over the interloping personality.

Cautiously, over the next fortnight, always on guard for "Mati," Sha Sha began to tell her story. When she was in the closet she had been back in her home in Mokhi Maya. Apparently, it had been her mother's custom to lock her in a small cabinet in the wall of their dwelling. When "Mati" became angry the child had learned to hide in the closet hoping to escape the mother's wrath.

As was the custom, one day the High Priestess had come with a small entourage to the child's home. The Priestess called the child to her and looked into her eyes for the longest time. Then she sighed and smiled, turning to her ministers and saying, "Yes, this is the one."

Sha Sha remembered how the Priestess picked her up and held her close, making her feel "all happy inside." In this manner had Sha Sha been selected by the Source to become the next High Priestess of the people of Mokhi Maya.

She was to remain at home under her parents' tutelage for the first few years of her life. Around the age of five, more extensive lessons would begin. She was to be trained in the history and customs of the priesthood that would assist her in bringing out her innate powers and gifts, and most importantly her connection with the universal forces which we simply referred to as the Source.

The child, Sha Sha, through the channeled mediumship of Susan, was encouraged to tell me about her "Mati" and how she had lived her early childhood in her "Mokhi Maya" home.

This was to become a process of discovering, revealing, and remembering; not only for the personalities of the soul that were involved, but also for one who would become the protector of a child priestess.

The Mokhi Maya Mati was very unhappy with the prospect of having to accept that she had become the mother of the next High Priestess. She was somewhat of a reclusive person who shunned public attention. There was not much interest or acceptance in the sacred teachings of the time. Mati was what we might call a profoundly secular person who found herself in the midst of a theocratic society that was abhorrent to every fiber of her recalcitrant being.

It was difficult, if not outright impossible, for her to accept the possibility of the divinity that was to shine forth through this little child that she had so unwillingly birthed. It was an anathema for her to even consider the possibility that something could be divine.

So, now she would be in the limelight. All eyes would be upon her, as the blessed vessel of a messenger of God whose only purpose was to offer guidance and counsel to a generation of an emerging culture. The child was to be one of a continuing line of those sent to inspire a people chosen to go forth and multiply, to secure the success of the sacred pilgrimage of pristine spirit that had wrapped itself into flesh bodies, bringing forth the manifestation of the God Head into an earthly dimension.

Bowing to the rage within her, this "Mokhi Maya" mother began to taunt and tease the child. She would tell the child that she was not really a priestess. She would tell her that she was a horrible creature and that she was evil. As evidence of this conclusion, Mati would point to the horrible stench of the putrid substances that would exude from the child's bowels. How could anything that smells so bad come from something that was supposed to be divine?

The child would not be changed and was forced to lie in her own excrement for days. Sometimes she would be starved. Attempts were even made to make her consume her own waste. Sometimes the child would be given poisonous concoctions with the rationalization that, if the child were really special, the tainted elixirs would not hurt her. When the child would cry or complain, she would be beaten and locked away from the prying eyes of neighbors.

In horror, the mother once saw pulsing white light coming out of the child's hands, which the Source said was a manifestation of the child's gift of healing. The Source explained that it had been the wish of the soul at a very deep level to reach out and to heal the anguish that was twisting this Mokhi Maya mother into the monster that she had become. But, the mother saw this as an attack upon her by some demonic force.

In seething fury, she grabbed a sharp implement and began cutting out the energies she saw coming from the child's hands.

The palms of Susan's hands were sometimes irritated by a fungal-like infection that made them look red and blistered. We learned that this was a lingering result of Sha Sha's Mokhi Maya mother attempting to cut out the light that was seen emanating from her hands.

I was in the habit of taking a pinch of earth or sand from the many sacred sites that we had visited during our pilgrimages and travels. The contents were kept in a small bottle and sometimes placed upon the altar that we had constructed at the Source's suggestion.

With the Source's direction, I took a pinch of this blended earth and mixed into it some oils making a sort of poultice. I rubbed it into her palms and within a few hours the blemishes disappeared and never appeared again.

Together we lived and relived a number of these tragic and traumatic moments, as they were remembered, relived, and healed.

The father was a very proud soul. He became unwilling, and therefore unable, to address the sickness that was welling up within the mother, destroying the family, and undermining the psychological fabric of the nation's anointed oracle.

The prospect of the humiliation of public disclosure was more than he could bear. He was as Joseph watching Mother Mary torture and violate the Christ Child. The more he saw and realized; the more he did not want to know. The agony of his dilemma eventually drove him into exile. In the beginning, he attempted to throw himself into his work in order to avoid the evil that pervaded his home.

He was one who worked as an expert and developer of the methods of growing food. It was necessary for him to travel throughout the empire, observing, learning, teaching, and mediating; thus enabling him to create the systems, practices, and hybrids that would afford those involved in agriculture the ability to be productive and fruitful to feed a growing nation.

Eventually, he left his people and wandered through the wilderness until he found an uneasy sanctuary somewhere on the other side of the great mountains where no one knew his name. He would discover new times and new places, finally finding a magical way to release himself of the burden that he has unnecessarily carried for so long.

Sha Sha had a big brother that she called Labhar. He was also very proud. He was exceedingly proud that he had the honor of being the elder brother of the Priestess. He felt tremendous guilt that he was unable to protect his Priestess from their deranged Mokhi Maya Mati.

This mother did not trust him. She was afraid he would tell. She saw an unrelenting strength in him that would be her undoing. She would send him on trips with his father, but after awhile he would refuse to go. If his father took him, he would run away and come back home to try and protect his little sister, the Priestess.

Mati would beat him repeatedly, but one day he responded to the mother's abuse and began attacking and kicking her with such conviction and ferocity that she never hit him again. After that, she would not hurt the child when Labhar was present. But young Labhar remained in a state of almost constant torment and shame that he was not able to do more to protect his Priestess, even though he was only nine years old when the abuse began.

All this and much more was the remembering of the story that the little one described; the story that the Source was imparting as more and more of the details of a lifetime in a distant culture slowly unraveled and came into focus.

Over and over again, we lived and re-experienced many of the torturous events that were to be suffered, understood, and overcome; yet, always in the presence and under the watchful guidance and protection of the Source.

Sha Sha's soul ached to be loved and accepted by her mother. She prayed and prayed that she would no longer be evil so that her mother would no longer hate her and be ashamed. One night, as I held her gently in my arms, she began sobbing, asking the Source to please forgive her for being so bad.

With great compassion, tears began to well up from the depths of my being. I realized that this precious little soul, so full of loving, so full of innocence was caught in an endless struggle to be forgiven so that her mother would accept her and "not have to hurt me anymore to make the evil go away."

Along with the tears, words welled up within me. "You are not the evil one. You are your Tati's most precious treasure. It is your Mati who is the evil one."

She looked up into my face with shock and disbelief. With her lips quivering, in a trembling little voice she responded, "I am a precious treasure?"

"Of course you are," I squeaked. "Are you not the one that the Source has chosen to speak to your people? Have you not listened and heard the wise and helpful words that are given through you? Have you not seen and felt the appreciation and wonder of those that receive the Babbling's messages?"

I told her that whatever evil that there might be was coming from her Mati, not from a tiny and precious little girl.

Slowly her eyes widened and brightened. She let loose a long, ragged sigh. Her countenance became joyful and her mood blissful. As with many abused children, she had not yet considered that it could be the parent that was the aberration. She had always assumed that everything was her fault, that everything her mother had said and done was justified.

She seemed surprised and a little relieved, when I told her that everyone sometimes has foul-smelling things coming out of their bodies and that is why we need to use the bathrooms. She was not quite sure if I was being truthful and had to think on this awhile.

I further explained that we all need diapers when we are little and it is our parents' duty to take care of us and keep us clean until we are able to take care of ourselves. I reminded her of the diapers in the stores. I pointed out how other Matis in our current time and place were caring for their young children. That seemed to satisfy her doubts.

Later that evening, after a long period of silence, the Source began to speak. I will not pretend to remember the exact words, but it went something like this:

We would that you could hear up into the heavenly realms, for there is great rejoicing. Behold! The angels themselves do sing!

Now the healing has begun. This is the purpose for which you were born; the reason you came into physical form at this time. And it could be accomplished by none other than the embodiment of those present in this room.

There would be other events such as this one, but they were quite pale by comparison. They were merely aftershocks of this one pivotal event that began the process of liberation for this once-upon-a-time, tormented little priestess.

Chapter 11

The Raising of a Priestess

The periodic pilgrimages continued; sometimes with the little priestess in tow, and sometimes with her leading the way. At the behest of the Source, the recorded sessions began to diminish. Eventually, they essentially became nonexistent, except for rare and extraordinary circumstances. This process began while we were visiting the Chaco Canyon Center in Northern New Mexico.

We were told that Chaco is one of the most ancient sites of human habitation on the planet. It was further explained that, through several different ages, a variety of people had returned to this site with the currently visible structures being the remains of the most recent cycle. Like many other sacred sites, these more recent people had returned due to what the Source termed "unconscious soul memory" and something referred to as "the physical cellular memory." This memory supposedly exists within many of the individuals that are drawn to the American Southwest.

These waves of returning pilgrims often built right on top of the previous ruins and structures. This is usually done unknowingly, since through the ages the more ancient temples and structures have deteriorated and become buried deep beneath the surface through natural erosion and cycles of climate change. The Source also indicated that some of the earlier civilizations were considerably more advanced than those that came later.

We were told that the areas between the little mesas were once deep canyons where water and wildlife had flourished in great abundance and had played a part in attracting the inhabitants. It was supposedly the first place where the ancient Hopis reached out and began their migratory process for the habitation of the planet.

Years later, I was to discover that an initial geologic survey was being conducted that had encountered ruins of much larger structures, which had existed deep below the current surface of the valley in Chaco. It was explained that this discovery was accomplished through sound imaging, which since then has become even more popular in both mineral exploration and archeology. Some of the discoveries were as much as forty feet below the current ground level.

I was told by a visiting park ranger that there will probably never be any excavation on what was found, because it would be too expensive to dig so deep and that many of the existing, more modern structures would be destroyed in the process. Of course, the modern indigenous people and a multitude of laws regarding antiquities would most likely not permit such a sacrilege. For us, this obvious technological proof was all that was required.

As we wandered through the desert, Hawk Woman burst forth and began chanting and intonating in a very soothing and mesmerizing manner. Later, the Source continued by describing the purposes, alignments, and functions of the huge structures that are currently preserved at the site. I had been abruptly asked to put the distraction of the recording device aside and to just listen, explore, and become aware of as much as was possible for me to experience. The little one emerged after Hawk Woman's performance and was disappointed that Tati was not able to "do remembering of the ancient times."

After some additional quiet wandering, the Source continued with its explanations. We were told that much of the information and many of the experiences that were being offered to "the channels" were given for the development of our own personal attunement and personal growth. It was expected that in time we would be able to have our own revelations without the need for intervention by the Source.

It was pointed out that many pilgrims had traversed into the sacred areas with a multitude of different experiences along with contrasting levels of comprehension. Each was having their own unique experiences and revelations, with all paths generally progressing in a parallel manner. But, as each would come and establish a personal connection and witnessing within the soul, the way would become easier. The experiences would become stronger for all who would come to celebrate the places where both the people and the land had been jointly anointed.

The forces expressing themselves through the channel were relentless in encouraging me to move through the simple meanings of words of the Source and to begin to feel, sense, and know through my own direct connection, my own revelations and experiences. As these phenomena began to manifest, there would often be a sort of debriefing or clarification of what it was that I had encountered.

While in the Chaco area, we were led to an unexcavated ruin on top of a little mesa where I was to sit alone and quietly meditate. It seemed like hours. Then, I began to see the dust from the dancing feet of dark-haired and brown-skinned people slowly moving around and around in a gigantic circle. There was much drumming and chanting. It was as if I had drifted off into a very vivid dream in another time and place.

I was supposedly bearing witness to a ceremonial practice that had existed for many generations. It was as if the land had absorbed the pious energies of an entire community in reverent celebration of the cycles of life as they slowly danced around a great circle in this ancient plaza. This blessing was now being released in waves of healing and bliss.

For a moment, I was given the blessing of being allowed to see it through what the child called "remembering." I was later told that sometimes you could even remember into the future.

I was brought back to a normal state of consciousness when something touched me on the forehead. It was Hawk Woman standing there in all her glory. For a brief moment I could see her original form in that first incarnation. This dear and beloved friend was truly magnificent. She seemed very pleased, nodding her approval at my accomplishment.

Without a word, we walked slowly back down a rocky trail overgrown with brown, brittle brush. The gentle howling wind and rustle of our steps was interrupted by occasional episodes of my little priestess singing and dancing with the kind of joy that is mostly reserved for the innocence of childhood. As I continued downward into the setting sun toward the Scout, I could still feel the monotonous beating of the drums. The primal pulsing lingered within the depths of my being well into the night.

Given the complexity of the circumstances, I shall always remain in awe at how Sha Sha fit right into the family. When I reflect back upon it, I am often amazed at how our children just accepted the whole process. It could be said that they simply considered her to be one of their siblings. They would sometimes play together and even squabble just like all young playmates do. Sha Sha enjoyed coloring and drawing, but she particularly enjoyed word games. She would spend hours looking over Mati

Susan's shoulder when court transcripts were being typed. Sometimes she liked to sit on her Mati Susan's lap and pretend to drive the car. Much to her disappointment, the Source would sometimes remove her from private conversations or block her from seeing questionable scenes in movies.

She did not often reveal herself outside of the family circle, and almost never to strangers. When she did present herself, folks were usually oblivious to what was happening; usually thinking Susan was perhaps just in a silly mood, not realizing the extent of what was before them.

Sha Sha, in the guise of Susan, loved to talk to children and the elderly. During those encounters she frequently delivered little messages of hope or inspiration that were being stealthily offered by the Source.

Once she was directed to tell a woman to contact a medical specialist, complete with phone number. The recipient was told that this particular physician might be able to address a very painful and chronic condition that had been wrestled with for several years. The lady seemed surprised, and a bit taken aback, that a complete stranger would know about her medical proclivities. Months later we encountered this lady again. She ran to Susan gushing with thanks. But it was Sha Sha who had carried the message. Apparently, she had followed the advice and was now in complete remission.

Another time, I found Sha Sha sitting on a bench in a restaurant with a very feeble woman who had tears in her eyes. The old woman was saying she had wanted to take a trip up on the mesa to see the aspen trees in autumn just one more time. The elderly lady had feared she didn't have much time left. Sha Sha, in Susan's voice, told her she had an angel with her who assured her she had more than enough time left to see the mesa again and they would make it happen.

If there was any potential for embarrassment or discomfort Sha Sha would straight away be absorbed back into a clear-thinking Susan who could usually continue the conversation without missing a beat. Outside of the family there were only four or five people who actually met Sha Sha or otherwise had any inkling that she had been in their presence. Whenever Susan had things she wanted or needed to do, the little one would automatically retreat into whatever realm of the psyche from which she had come.

In this manner the little one would watch and learn about the people, the culture and what kinds of things Susan needed to be doing. This was done most often with the blessing and encouragement of the Source. Always the Source seemed to be in charge as a benevolent force or guardian, overseeing the entire process; capable of stopping or redirecting it at any time. It seemed to serve as a sort of governor, always keeping Susan and her intra-psychic offspring out of any serious social or physical jeopardy.

Over time a whole protocol developed around the social interactions of this little Priestess from Mokhi Maya. When we would go out to eat or in other social situations we would seek out a booth where we could face each other; Susan would usually face the wall. In this manner no one in the room could see her facial expressions except me. This afforded the opportunity for the little one to come forth, complete with her transforming smiles, giggles, and looks of wonder as she studied and observed our culture.

On occasion Hawk Woman would look in, serving as a sort of grandmother. Sometimes there would be some playful teasing, which was quite an accomplishment for an old bird that originally emerged with absolutely no sense of humor. Her severe countenance, as I used to call it, was the result of much heartache and trauma from that first incarnation that was supposedly being ameliorated by the current associations within the body and psyche of my beloved Susan.

Hawk Woman was fond of offering a whimsical frown, a grunt, or even a sort of gutteral chirp with head slightly tilting and bobbing, just so we might know that the "feathered presence" was in residence. At other times, she might break in with an insightful observation or a word from the so-called universal Source with which she too, of course, was quite familiar and adept.

During one period lasting for several weeks, usually during morning meditations, the feathered presence would intermittently erupt with her sacred chantings, some of which would come with an esoteric explanation and an invitation for me to participate. She seemed dismayed that my "advanced" yoga was so primitive and fraught with superstition; but, she seemed pleased that, at least, we still know something about it.

At other times, she would simply burst forth with a set of rather resonant, high pitched intonations resembling the chirping or screeching of a winged predator.

Little Sha Sha was very impressed by this and started imitating the sounds as she would run wildly around the house, sometimes flapping her arms like wings and pretending that she could fly. How these sounds were ever produced by Susan's voice box I do not know. The children would try to mimic Sha Sha and she would try to teach them, but to no avail. It was a talent that, thankfully, they were unable to learn. Once, Sha Sha told us that she had found baby Hawk Woman and seemed absolutely mystified that we were unable to see her playmate who was allegedly standing right beside her.

Our daughter started calling Sha Sha the "squeaky priestess." This seemed to encourage more of the same behavior. The screeches became very loud and piercing and would tend to make us cover our ears in the hopes of avoiding painful attacks on our fragile eardrums.

Susan began chastising the child, trying to get her under control. But every so often out would come an excruciating screech leaving us with our ears ringing, as the little one laughed and giggled. Although the child continued to be amused, the novelty soon lost its luster.

One afternoon, I returned home from a day of showing real estate to find a wife who was unable to speak. Susan shoved a note at me with an explanation. Apparently, Susan's voice had been temporarily paralyzed by the Source in order to keep the little one from abusing it. She was getting out of control and not being a very good guest; Sha Sha was not being respectful of Mati Susan and the temple—the body—that she was being allowed to inhabit.

We were told she was being taken to a place where the child would receive "appropriate adjustments." After a few hours the voice returned, but the child was gone for almost a month.

Visiting and living in this modern era took its toll on the little Priestess. When first she came, her psychic abilities seemed strong and profound. But as the years progressed the abilities apparently diminished. The Source said it was due to the growing maturation process and the inhibitions of a denser physical form, Susan's physical body.

When Sha Sha first arrived, she could see auras and ghostly spirits quite clearly. She knew what animals were experiencing and what was troubling them. There was the ability to look at the physical body and supposedly see energy lines and blockages. Sometimes she would stick out her little finger and with no warning jam it into a particular lymph node or pressure point, thus relieving blockages and inducing physical well-being.

The unsuspecting recipient of these healthful attacks would often burst out in moans and groans that were both agony and ecstasy. The little one delighted in practicing her trade. I was often a happy recipient of her special therapy. She could soothe tired, sore muscles, reconfigure a strained back, or dispatch a migraine headache in a manner of seconds.

Apparently, she was just chasing away the sad looking light that she saw coming from some parts of the body. When she was a healer, her hands would get so warm they would start to turn red. Sometimes she would sweat profusely. It was not uncommon for her to take upon herself the particular pains and discomforts that her patient was feeling. It was as if the energies would pass from your body through hers and then be released.

She claimed to be able to see colors and energies emanating from food. Some foods had very little or no light around it. At first she would refuse to eat it. The more vibrant food was referred to as "real food." The Source confirmed that what the child was seeing was correct. Some foods have life-giving energies and some actually act as a sponge and absorb life-giving energy from the body.

The child loved to be surrounded by statues and pictures of Mary, mother of Jesus. However, she always called her rendition of this archetype Hawk Mati (Hawk Mother). Sometimes she would stare upward as if in a trance with a very delighted look on her face and later tell me that her Hawk Mati had come to visit her.

Shopping was hard for my little intra-psychic daughter. She would look at the all the frilly, brightly colored little girl clothes at the department stores. It was difficult for her to understand why her Tati couldn't buy her some little girl clothes. She would hold up the little girl dresses and clutch them to her body, trying to imagine what it would be like if she could wear them. Eventually, she would remember that she was a visitor in a big lady's body that was my wife—a lady she looked to as the good mother, her Mati Susan.

I will always wonder if she ever fully understood the situation. Perhaps none of us will ever truly understand that bizarre situation. But at the time, after the initial shock, it all seemed as natural as breathing.

Eventually, Sha Sha did become somewhat comfortable with the idea that the body was like a "dolly" and that for some silly reason the Babbling (Source) was having her share it with Mati Susan. She became very concerned when she realized that her Tati could not see her in her Mokhi Maya body. Several times she brought me greeting cards with images of long-haired, brown-faced little Indian girls. Sometimes she would spend hours drawing a special picture so that I might know what she looked like. She lamented the fact that she couldn't draw as well as her Mati Susan; but Susan, after all, was a trained sketch artist.

The little lady became quite well adapted to modern technology. She was a good shopper and intuitively knew just what gift would be both appropriate and appreciated. She loved to buy presents. She began telling me about this place she went when I was gone where all these nice ladies would talk to her and show her things.

Being busy with the typical householder tasks of the day I didn't pay much attention to it. Until one day Susan asked me if I had been ordering things through the mail. It turned out that by watching Susan she had discovered the wonderful world of gift-giving by means of a television shopping channel and a credit card.

Actually, we kept most of the stuff. They were mostly rather superb and thoughtful Christmas gifts. After that, all shopping had to be done with Mati Susan or Tati present. She agreed, at least for a little while. When the bills would come, Sha Sha would wail and lament that she didn't understand money and she wished she could just go back to Mokhi Maya.

On one occasion, the child emerged and presented herself as being quite intoxicated. She laughed and giggled incessantly, was slurring her words, and staggered across the room, finally collapsing on the floor with a marked loss of fine motor control. Then, she started crying and obviously felt very ashamed and embarrassed. After a little sobering up, she told us a story with the help of the Source. Apparently, she had been in Mokhi Maya and was to be present at an informal gathering of the leaders and elders of the time.

There was one particular participant who was quite envious of the little Priestess. It was a woman of the Priest Clan lineage who had given birth to a female child on the same day that Sha Sha was born. Apparently, she had questioned and petitioned the elders and the High Priestess, asserting that perhaps it was her child who was the anointed one, suggesting that there must have been some kind of error or misinterpretation.

There were in existence at that time certain hallucinogenic substances that were sparingly used as a part of certain ceremonies for the purpose of expanding the consciousness, usually during rites of initiation. The substances were considered to be very sacred. The recipe and its preparation was a highly guarded secret. The formula was given by the Source. It was something that was not recommended for this time and place.

It was to be used at the sole discretion of certain members of the Priest Clan. There was concern that haphazard or recreational use among the population could become a detriment to the culture, rather than a helpful adjunct to be used sparingly only during very specific types of instruction and training.

Sha Sha referred to the substance as "herb juice." She told us that she had unknowingly been given the herb juice by the envious mother. The plan was to embarrass and discredit the little Priestess in public; thereby adding credence to the claim that it was this other woman's child, not Sha Sha, who was to be the next High Priestess.

The High Priestess supposedly took Sha Sha in her arms, carrying her into her chambers where she could be properly attended. The aberrant mother was quietly escorted out of the temple city. There, she was searched and questioned in order to determine how she had gained access to the elixir.

Apparently, the plot was clearly exposed and Sha Sha's legitimacy was never in doubt. However, the child was very upset and embarrassed about the whole incident.

One morning the little one ran up to me all excited and squealing with joyful tears. She told me that the big Priestess had come to see her. She came with a lot of special people right to her house to visit her and to see if she was all right. Sha Sha said that Mati had been very nervous for several days. The child had been dressed in her best clothes, and neighbors had been bringing food and gifts. She did not know why until the High Priestess arrived at the door.

At this point in her story, Sha Sha looked sad and burdened, almost panicky as she related that she was afraid she could never be a very good priestess. I reminded her of the night I found her in the closet and reassured her that the Source had chosen her and I had no doubt that, although things might be difficult at times, that there was no question that she was worthy.

She looked at me with wonder and said "Labhar, that is what the Priestess came to be saying to me." Sha Sha described the Priestess as being angry with her Mokhi Maya Mati. She said they went outside for a long walk and there was a lot of talking. When they came back, Mati looked very afraid and would not look at anyone. The exasperated Sha Sha exclaimed, "Well, Tati, you should know all about it. You were there when you were big brother, Labhar."

The Priestess then took my little Sha Sha for a walk. The child related how they rolled in the grass, laughed and giggled, and did all kinds of silly things, pretending to fly, to walk like animals, and to swim like fish. She said the Priestess picked her up and held her very tight for a very long time and she got "big happy tears in her eyes." The lady was described as very old, but very beautiful.

Sha Sha said the Priestess told her that no one truly knows what it is like to be the Priestess, except another priestess. She told the little one that for a short time when one priestess is old and the other is young, they can visit each other and be friends. She told the child she should always make time for "being silly," as the little one called it.

The Priestess had said that this is what the previous priestess had told her when she was little, and they too made time to be silly and play together. It was a very eventful day, which made a big impression on all in attendance, especially Sha Sha and her "Mokhi Maya Mati."

Chapter 12

The Dolly Hits the Wall

The child often exhibited considerable fear when riding in automobiles. When she first experienced our modern miracles of transportation she would push herself back in the seat and hold her arms out straight, as if to brace herself for eminent impact.

Sometimes she would contort her face and look quite terrified. At first, she would emerge intermittently, remaining for brief, fleeting periods of time. After a few short episodes of this behavior, she eventually became adequately accustomed to riding in our Scout, but with a few twists.

One spring day when we were driving to Montrose for shopping, she was exposed to a rather gruesome corpse of a deer that had been hit by a car and left to rot on the side of the road. It was quite upsetting for her. After that, whenever we would travel through deer country she would put all five of her little fingers together and pray most earnestly, hoping that deer would stay away from our vehicle and remain safe.

This was something that the Source taught her to do. I noted that her positioned fingers strongly resembled a white-tantric mudra that I had been exposed to in my quest to master Kundalini yoga. The gesture made her feel a little more relaxed and in control. I don't know if this ritual ever had any direct influence; but in all our years of dodging frenzied deer, we never hit one.

She called the deer, "darsiri" and explained that this was the name they were given in Mokhi Maya. After that initial incident, it seemed that whenever we would pass a dead or injured deer along the road she would be unable to see it. It was as if she had been hypnotized, perhaps by the Source, and given a negative suggestion so that she didn't have to endure the trauma of ever seeing another fallen darsiri. She once told me that in Mokhi Maya she would call to them and they would come to visit her.

Although she eventually got over it, she was very embarrassed when we had to explain that the short, fat darsiri she had discovered was actually a different kind of animal that we call a cow. Through the years we were graced with the opportunity to share many discoveries in our world through the eyes of a little Priestess who had come to visit us from another time and place.

She always had this tendency toward what some call an exaggerated startle response. Her behavior seemed somewhat consistent with some kind of event resulting in a post traumatic stress disorder. In Susan's life there didn't seem to be any known precipitating event that might explain these reactions.

However, if there was a lot of traffic closing in from other lanes, or if we followed other vehicles too closely, she could become a quite panicked. She didn't like to see anything thrown or moving rapidly past her. Even Susan had a tendency to get a bit agitated if the kids and I would toss something around the house in the course of some playful mischief.

One very eventful day, Susan was in the crowded little office on the second floor next to the kitchen. She had been working on the computer all morning trying to catch up on a transcript that had to do with a lawsuit over an Arizona train derailment. It was time for a break. She had just made a couple of phone calls and we were thinking of going down to the Floradora for lunch. All of a sudden, there was a long unintelligible groan. Then she yelled out.

"Did you hear that? Didn't you hear that? It was so loud. A noise, like a big bang, or thump. No, it was more like a crack! You must have heard it!"

I hadn't heard anything.

She seemed a bit disoriented and annoyed that I did not hear it. She started complaining about a huge headache and then gasped, "O my god ..."

Next, she stumbled into the living room and collapsed on the floor like a rag doll. Her breathing became labored and erratic. Her eyes started to flutter and her body began contorting and twitching like she was having a seizure. It stopped almost as soon as it started. Now she was just laying there, still and lifeless.

It all happened so quickly. I was thinking about trying to check to see if she was breathing and could be aroused. In panic, my eyes began searching for the phone on the counter while I struggled to remember who I should call for help.

Kneeling at her side, I suddenly felt the presence of a huge hand on my left shoulder. It was warm and heavy. But, no one was there. I realized I was paralyzed, unable to move or even to think.

Then a voice, presumably belonging to the hand, said, "No! Wait!"

After what seemed like an eternity, she groaned out a shallow, ragged breath. She sat up. Cautiously, she looked around the room, rubbing her eyes and stretching like someone just waking from a long deep sleep.

It was Sha Sha. With a tiny little voice, she began to speak. "Mati broke my bowl. She was mad at me and threw it against the wall."

She was staring into space, squinting inquisitively as if she were trying to see something. "No," she explained, "Babbling says the bowl is my head. It's broken. Mati threw baby against the wall. And there, (pointing) is my dolly [the child's body]. It's all broken. Mati is really scared."

The Source explained that the child was out of her body in Mokhi Maya and was observing her still, lifeless body lying on the floor. Her mother had supposedly erupted in rage when the child refused to eat the food that had been prepared for her.

Sha Sha was afraid to eat for fear that it might hurt her stomach; her Mokhi Maya Mati was once more torturing the child by mixing toxic and putrid ingredients into her meals.

I held her close and suggested that this might be a good time to put her fingers together and talk to the Babbling to try and get the attention of the Priestess so that she might be able to hear her and come to help. She prayed and prayed, a most beautiful and soulful prayer. I held her close; trembling, feeling angry and helpless, as she sobbed and sobbed.

After awhile she fell asleep in my arms sucking her thumb. I put her to bed, carefully adjusted her pillows and tucked her in, just the way she liked.

If memory serves me right, I somehow got the Roma to deliver some pizza for dinner. I explained to the family that Susan wasn't feeling well and that everyone should stay downstairs while she rested. Mollie kept sneaking up the stairs; she couldn't stop walking back and forth, constantly pushing her loose glasses back up on her nose. She kept telling me not to worry; everything would be all right. Mollie often comforted herself by telling others that everything would be all right.

A couple of times the baby woke up. I gave her water and some fruit and cheese which she daintily chewed, while making sure I had some too.

Once she told me, "It's okay, Tati Labhar. Babbling loves us and will always take care of us."

Spoken like a true Priestess, I thought to myself. Somewhere inside of me I could feel a big brother with a heart that was breaking and a soul full of shame. He felt so responsible. Part of Labhar's mission was to be the elder brother—the protector of the Priestess, his baby sister. It was not clear to me which child was injured more profoundly.

At that time, it was very clear to me that the Priestess and her big brother had indeed returned from somewhere beyond the great veil. If there ever was any doubt, it was now gone. We had returned and we were still together and I resolved that no one was ever going to hurt her again, though I really didn't know how to make that a reality.

It's the kind of boastful thing that you often say when you feel completely helpless. It might make you feel better, but it is a lie; no one is that powerful. I quietly watched over my Priestess until the early morning hours when I too fell asleep.

The next morning we went to Sofios for a big breakfast. By now, in Mokhi Maya, the High Priestess had hurriedly arrived. The child had died. We were told that through divine intervention she had been revived. And, somehow, through the healing arts of the time she was kept alive, but was brought back to lay in a coma, unaware of her immediate surroundings.

But we knew where she was. She was with her Tati Labhar in the sacred mountains that she called Adnipoche—in Telluride, the sacred valley.

Sha Sha would break in here and there and provide firsthand descriptions and additions to the narrative that the Source patiently provided. The little one had been taken to a place she called The Temple of Healing. No doubt a term plucked from Susan's conscious mind, taken from the Cayce readings that we had studied so many years before.

The mother was taken into custody and kept under guard. She supposedly wailed hysterically and was eventually taken to "a closely watched community with others of similar challenges."

The father, full of guilt and shame, never returned. He heard of the incident while he was away in another province. It was his assumption that the child had perished. But he, too, would eventually find his own path back to his own Mokhi Maya.

Again, all that is yet another story; just one more little story of the many stories—all woven together into the tapestry of the one big story that evolves into the magic that is our human sojourn.

Meanwhile, the entire Priest Clan, all the healers, worked their craft. The people fasted and prayed for the recovery of the little lady who was born to be their next High Priestess. The little Priestess continued to lay in a coma for several days.

Eventually, she was revived. She was presented to the people by the High Priestess in a special ceremony so that everyone could celebrate her recovery. Sitting on the lap of the High Priestess, who was borne on a sedan chair, she was taken to a great banquet and celebration. This was an important public display; it was seen as a reaffirmation of her birthright. Some saw it as a sort of miraculous resurrection and proof of her divine mission; a display of the power of the Source that remained alive within her and within their community.

Yet, it was still hard to understand why one such as this would be born to a woman who found the child to be such an anathema. To her Mokhi Maya Mati, giving birth to a child such as this was not an honor or blessing; but rather an insidious nightmare orchestrated by all that she found repugnant. It was a visceral thing that wrenched up from the core of the mother's being. To her, it was like God turned to Satan, invading the most sacred part of her body and laughing in her face.

We were taught that the souls that became human and inhabited the earth arrived in several waves. It was also explained that, during this current end time, we are now experiencing another onslaught of newly arriving souls. It is my understanding that many of the old souls that came during the initial waves may soon be leaving. As the cycle completes itself and "comes around twice," they shall be afforded the opportunity to return to the spirit world from whence they came.

These original souls, of the primal wave, of several small groupings, were essentially here since the formation of the planet itself. Actually, some of these declined physical entry and sometimes serve as guardians of the entry portals of the planet.

A second entry of souls emerged in the quest to explore and maintain the balance in the domain of the worldly. Many of these came as volunteer emissaries to lift the veil of forgetfulness, right any wrongs, and continue the divine connection with the greater universe from which we have all sprung. It was the dominant prerogative of these later descending souls to attempt to retain the sacred connection with their godhead and thus infuse and reintroduce a sense of harmony and cooperation into this evolving human drama of this alien earthly realm. They had come for their own purposes, but also to serve as a bridge for the return of others, of the first entry, who could no longer find the way back to the divine realms on their own.

These are the ones the Source referred to generically as "The Priest Clan," or as more recent scripture has expressed it, "the one-hundred-and-forty-four thousand," ones who were chosen at their inceptions by choosing themselves and by answering the halcyon cries of their lost and suffering brothers and sisters. Some of these have succeeded remarkably. Others have succumbed and also wander in the great darkness, while the light of creation still lingers within them, waiting to be rediscovered and reconnected.

Later, during the third entry, there was another continuing, massive influx of souls; souls that were also becoming curious, captivated, and reveling in the splendor that could be experienced within this earthly realm. These would come from many alternate dimensions and realities, but all having in common a desire to explore and inhabit the earth.

During another circumstance, a fourth entry of souls began to manifest.

As this fourth entry began to move away from the conscious presence of God and into the spirit world, and then into the carnal realms, they began to experience a tremendous sense of disappointment and torment.

Many of these souls came to believe that they had been needlessly manipulated and cast out. They could not see, or would not accept, their own decisive participation in the process of becoming human and moving into the flesh world.

Feeling the great anger of betrayal, they sought to rebel from a creator that they believed had ruthlessly abandoned them—leaving them in the earth to fend for themselves. They decided to rebel and reject the divine, setting themselves up as the final authority and never again bowing to any heavenly master.

God no longer had anything to do with them. He had become their enemy. He would not recognize them as His people; and they would not recognize him as their God. At the soul level, this is the way they tended to see their circumstances.

Completely rebelling, rejecting the divine, they wished to rely solely and wholeheartedly on their own individual abilities, talents, and insights, with no thought of the consequences to themselves or others.

As their divine consciousness began to wane they would learn to twist this agony into a great anger, a viciousness that calls for a relentless revenge. Thus emerged a lust for control, domination, self-aggrandizement, and a recalcitrant position of almost endless dissention. Some refer to this as the Enemy Way.

All of these various groupings began their involvement in the astral and spirit realms long before actually inhabiting flesh bodies. Their interests and proclivities developed and evolved at different times. They would actually arrive in the earth at various intervals, depending upon that which they had set in motion and ultimately chosen to experience once the cycles of incarnation had begun.

Thus, through the developing psyche of these earthbound beings and their evolving cultures came an infiltration of beings, both conscious and oblivious, that were intent upon the destruction of anything that might have even a hint of anything holy or sacred.

Such is the nature of the archetype that would unfold and manifest itself. Therefore, a great rift was opened within this community that a little Priestess called Mokhi Maya. In some teachings this process became known as the battle between the Children of the Darkness and the Children of the Light.

Of course, in the endgame, all would hopefully return to a perfect balance. For the light is unknown unless there is a contrasting presence of darkness. And darkness cannot be seen with out the contrasting brilliance of light. In truth, one does not exist without the other. Through time, the pendulum swings back and forth between these seemingly oppositional poles. It is a part of what it means to exist in this plane.

If the balance is ever achieved for even a mere moment, the duality in its destructive nature shall exist no more. We shall then "walk between the raindrops" and return completed, to the realm of spirit from whence we came.

But this was the process by which humankind began to infiltrate and influence the earth. This was the model that the souls developed and embraced. This is the friction necessary to induce the presence of creation: the positive and the negative, the yin and the yang.

This earthly dissention is nothing new. This battle, this rift, had erupted in the spirit world long before the embodiment of souls in the earth had even begun. The stresses and conflicts can sometimes be seen reflected and identified right into the veritable core of the planet, replete with geologic upheavals, eruptions, and a host of other destructive, polarizing calamities.

But all that is far beyond the scope of this one, simple little story.

So, when Hawk Woman first incarnated, she came as a teacher, imbued with the desire and the power to strengthen the community through the harmonious nurturance of children, family, and clan. Souls already here became jealous of the almost immediate recognition of the power, wisdom, and influence that was spontaneously afforded her in the community.

To souls that saw themselves as fallen, betrayed and abandoned, she represented all that they had rebelled against and were trying to forget. They hoped to become free, independent, and unencumbered by rules they believed they had no role in forming and did not agree with or understand. To them, Hawk Woman became an anathema. By her mere presence she was their enemy. A contingent arose, jealous of her influence and power. And they sought to destroy her.

So what did this have to do with the little Priestess, Sho Adh Shahannah? When this ancient soul decided to reincarnate in the place she referred to as Mokhi Maya, she chose to be born of the Matriarch that had once tricked her and led her to believe her children had perished. For as Susan had once been Sho Adh Shahannah, so had Sho Adh Shahanah been Hawk Woman in that first physical incarnation.

Sho Adh Shahannah was offering herself, in a state of grace, completely helpless and vulnerable to the Matriarch who had been the avenue for so much of her misery in that first incarnation. This was one soul offering another soul yet one more opportunity to learn to serve one another and to work together in harmony for the greater good of the community.

But it was too much for the Mokhi Maya Mati to bear. For her, it was as if she had given birth to the Antichrist. Not so much consciously but deep within her psyche, even unto the soul level, she could sense it—this intrusion, this insult of the so-called divine that had so inextricably abandoned her.

Sha Sha's Mati could not find the blessing or the grace in it. So, tragically, the little Priestess suffered, suffered profoundly even unto death in an attempt to forge some kind of reconciliation between the two: an attempt to heal the ancient rift between the ancient opposing matriarchs, one of which she had been—the one we now called Hawk Woman.

The Source concluded this revelation by explaining that, even though the effort might be seen by some as an abject failure, in truth this was not so. Now, having suffered so much, the little Priestess had been given the opportunity to learn from her travail and develop great compassion and insight into the suffering and trauma of others. If she could overcome such a tragic, cruel childhood and choose the way of righteousness rather than the way of revenge, she could become the greatest Priestess of them all.

The assault on the child became a revealing, a witness not just to the evil that is always present, but also a witness to the divine, which can ever redeem, even in the darkest hour. It is a condition that is the foundation of each human psyche as it wanders through its own episodes crucifixion and resurrection.

And in this process it might also be possible to assuage the guilt and shame of the soul who was the little one's brother, by affording him yet another opportunity to once more stand by his Priestess and safely deliver her, intact, to the Mokhi Maya nation that she had come to serve.

You see, this Labhar had been Hawk Woman's companion and helpmeet. He had been husband and father of her several children during that first incarnation in which the souls together bit into the earth and accepted the experience of inhabiting flesh bodies.

Thus was their descent into the earth, for both had been soundly duped and betrayed by their own lack of faith. They had accepted the lie that Hawk Woman's children had perished; when in truth it was a relatively simple task to discover that this was not so. But, it did require some faith, just a little hope, to at least ask.

Now, both of us had been given the opportunity to look into the eyes of the dragon, facing our fear, rage, guilt, and despair. We had experienced a great revealing.

Perhaps now would come a time for healing.

Chapter 13

Retreat from the Mountain

A fter several years of adventures and revelations within the San Juan Mountains we were entreated to leave the sacred valley. It seemed that all the drama and travail of my personal apprenticeship on the mountain was nearing completion. But again, all that is yet another story; just one more little story of the many stories: all woven together into the tapestry of the one big story that evolves into the magic that is our human journey.

It was time to transition into the next phase of a life of many unexpected and miraculous events. I reluctantly bowed to the inevitable. The Source wished us to remain in the Four Corners region and offered three possible locations where we might consider relocating. One by one, we made pilgrimages to the suggested communities. Eventually, we selected a new home near Grand Junction, Colorado.

We found a place in the suburbs where the regimentation of city living had not quite encroached. It is nestled next to a mesa with a maze of numerous enchanted canyons, replete with red rock spires and volcanic outcroppings. Though some call it the Colorado National Monument, the Source called it Zimba Aba-avache. Apparently, that was what it was once called by some long forgotten people who inhabited this place long before the advent of this modern era.

It is a terrain of tall trees, hardy grasses, and sandy, red soil. The water table is close to the surface. When first homesteaded, orchards flourished, but as economic conditions evolved the fruit trees were abandoned. Most died and were removed. A few hearty old cottonwoods stand as giant sentries, left behind from the original outposts that vanished during the last generation.

The land was once more revitalized with prolific wild elm and olive trees, with tall clumps of buffalo grass filling in the remaining open spaces. Now there is the careful coaxing of fragile vines of grapes from freshly prepared fields, as a fledgling wine industry struggles to take hold.

The house seemed huge at first. It was a two-story structure with dramatic cathedral ceilings throughout the first floor. Our son ruled the upstairs while we luxuriated in what seemed like an immense master bedroom. As the years went by the house was remodeled and updated. It has become a secluded, but not isolated sanctuary.

Here and there are ponds, both constructed and natural, where nurturing water percolates through sandy soil to offer life to what would otherwise be an arid desert. Coveted irrigation water is available to help keep the remaining pastures and orchards green, growing, and productive.

Close by, on the mesa, varieties of cedar and pinion rise up from the steep canyons and onto the rocky highlands. You can hear the coyotes howling at night as they prowl about during their nightly vigils. It is a moderate western climate for both winter and summer, but celebrates all the glory of four distinct seasons. It is a place of pheasants, geese, hawks, and an occasional wild turkey. The area may even offer a rare glimpse of a black bear or mountain lion.

It is a favorite hangout for deer, hiding among the brush and tall grass next to the cooling shade of the matted branches of untrimmed trees. Sometimes the darsiri like to graze in the pastures right next to a neighbor's horses, or among cattle brought in from the mountain ranges to wait out the winter.

Of course, there are a few ringtailed raccoons, squirrels, muskrats, and skunks. It is a good place for dogs and feral cats, provided that they don't startle the skunks.

You can sit out on the deck at night and listen to gurgling water trickling through irrigation pipes and ditches. If the gnats and mosquitoes are not too bad, you can linger awhile, basking in the majesty of the moon with all its accompanying heavenly bodies—just as God had intended—without the intrusion of crowds, traffic, and streetlights.

We discovered all this within fifteen minutes of the largest mall between Salt Lake City and Denver. The obscure listing, of course, was "suggested" by the Source; claiming "... all has been arranged. It is waiting for you."

As yet, there are no covenants and the neighbors get along well, but it seems that there are more of them all the time. Each new home is built a little larger than the last one. Each new construction project results in fewer trees and a little more pavement.

I finally gave in to the evolving times and imprisoned our two little acres with a "proper fence." The Nordic sweat lodge still stands beneath two old weeping willow trees, but I don't seem to use it much anymore.

I know that someday the road will be paved and streetlights will erupt. We will be annexed and I will have to move on; down the road to a new destination. But for now, it is truly a little slice of paradise.

I landed a position at the local social services agency. Following the coerced trail of political correctness, it changed its name to human services and then to community services. They probably call themselves something else by now. I found myself working as a case manager in the child protective services section, with adolescents mostly. How would you like to be a case manager with the Source in your ear every now and then, just to make sure the right folks ended up in the right places? Of course, I never put the source of those recommendations into in the treatment plans.

On the side, I continued to dabble in real estate. It eventually turned out to be a somewhat profitable hobby. But I am getting ahead of myself.

After much deliberation, we allowed our daughter to live with some friends and finish her senior year in Telluride. I didn't think she would make it. I thought she would eventually want to come and be with the family, but she stuck it out and graduated with honors. She did spend the summer with us after her high school graduation, before going off to college.

She still refers to her last year in Telluride as the time when her parents ran away from home. I was not ready for her to go—to be all grown up and on her own. But, she proved to be more than ready and capable. She now has a family of her own and I am called grandpa.

My son graduated a few years later. We spent a lot of time with Boy Scouts and a local Search and Rescue unit. They were good years and I will always treasure them. Now, he too has his own family. Susan and I are fortunate. Both our children grew up to be people we are proud to know.

Meanwhile, life continued on with the intermittent presence of our little priestess. We had become foster parents of a troubled little soul that spent a childhood with us that lasted almost twenty years. She was so full of magic and insight. I shall never be able to adequately describe what it was like to be in her presence.

If it were not for one or two friends who also knew her well, I might question if I had somehow made it all up; or was simply the observer of the manifestations of a tortured and deranged soul. But every word of her story is true. Her life was as real as any other I have known. There were so many things that happened, day to day, year to year. I will never be able to remember them all. But from time to time something will trigger a memory and I will smile, laugh, or maybe become a little tearful as I reflect upon my little Priestess of Mokhi Maya.

As our children began to mature, the little one would present herself to them less and less. It seemed like a good idea to allow our naturally born children some space and distance from this incredibly intricate and sometimes awkward situation. At times, it brought them considerable questioning and confusion: to have a little sister, who came from another time and place, a person they could not see that lived within their mother.

Though there was some occasional doubt on everyone's part, including Susan's, I did notice through the years that the children would often seek the council of the Source, even if at times they were not always aware of who was actually speaking. And every so often they would want to sort of check in to see how Sha Sha was doing.

Once again it seemed that this thing we called the Source, that the little one called "the Babbling," was ever watchful and in control; a stalwart guardian orchestrating some complex plan much of which, we were told, we would never fully comprehend or understand.

Sha Sha had been five years old for many years. Once we even had a birthday party for her. Of course, she had her own Christmas stocking and always got a few small presents, although she preferred to give presents rather than receive them. As time went by, she was becoming concerned that everyone else was getting older, but she was always five years old.

Then, a momentous thing happened just north of that place in Flagstaff. It was near the place where Hawk Woman first began to emerge. The ruins at Wapatki in Northern Arizona were one of the old bird's favorite places. If the Source would allow it, she could wander around for hours, supposedly remembering a previous sojourn.

Once, we were asked to stop the car so that Hawk Woman could stroll about the countryside. She walked slowly with great elegance and poise. She gazed knowingly over the landscape and then explained that she was visiting that same location in another time in the future. She wanted to precisely remember what it looked like before the return of the great waters, which we understood would eventually be an encroaching sea.

But this day was a day for Sha Sha. Hawk Woman had not been in residence for well over a year, maybe longer. A very dignified young lady touched my arm and said, "Tati, Babbling wants me to tell you something. After today you will never see me again. I am going to a place with the angels for more training and a special ceremony. The next time you see me I will be much older. We will never be five years old again. They are telling me that I am graduating to a different time."

We never heard from five-year-old Sha Sha again.

In her place soon emerged an older and much more serious version of the Priestess of Mokhi Maya. We came to call her "Big Sister," for she was obviously still Sha Sha and seemed to have all of her memories, but she had skipped a number of years. I would guess she was usually somewhere around twelve years old.

Then, a younger version of the Priestess emerged, much younger than five. Not more than two or three. This one became known as the "Baby Self." These two would function in tandem for the rest of their time with us.

During this phase the elder, Big Sister, Priestess became more and more of a caretaker and even a mother figure for this little one. It was as if Sha Sha were learning how to nurture and care for herself.

The Source explained that what I was witnessing was a part of the process of reintegration. It was explained that, at times, it could become quite emotional and I should be prepared for it. However, they reassured us that, although there is ever the choice, all was progressing quite satisfactorily.

There was one episode in which Susan was absent for well over two weeks. The one we called Big Sister was able to mimic much of Susan's speech and mannerisms. She was carrying on Susan's day-to-day responsibilities, appearing as if everything was normal. Sometimes I found myself forgetting, or rather attempting to ignore this somewhat uncomfortable situation.

As we went about our usual conversation, I occasionally found myself becoming annoyed with the things that were coming out of Susan's mouth. Things she supposedly didn't understand or couldn't remember. There were irritating, odd, and ignorant questions about things that were quite common and routine.

Then, I would once again realize that Susan was still gone and I was continuing to converse with a pubescent child who was trying to pass for an adult, in a foreign age and culture. I would get an uneasy feeling and have to put aside the denial that wasn't quite working for me.

I was becoming more than a little concerned, but there wasn't much I could do about it. Where had Susan gone? Was she somehow watching and unable to respond, or was she truly absent? Would she ever be back? Did anyone else notice that her behavior was a bit unusual? How long could the little one keep up this charade, even with the presumed "divine assistance?"

Who could I consult that could provide any reliable expertise with phenomenon such as this? Certainly, not the cadre of "professionals" I had worked with during the various facets of my career. However, the Source continued to be intermittently reassuring. So it seemed there was nothing to do but trust and wait and see what was going to happen next.

One day the Baby Self erupted and was quite upset. She had her hands on her hips and was puffing out her cheeks with angry tears in her eyes. She told me that Mati Susan had gone to Mokhi Maya and was pretending to be the Priestess.

Sha Sha was feeling very betrayed and was thinking that the Source had decided that she was not good enough to be the next Priestess. After some persistent consoling, she eventually began to calm down. About that time, Susan firmly emerged once more. She seemed incredibly energized and refreshed. She looked ten years younger.

At first, she was a bit confused, but it didn't seem to bother her. She couldn't recall what had happened or where she had been. Imagine what it might be like to wake up from a long sleep or have a blackout that lasted almost three weeks. Realizing she had been absent for awhile, she began surveying the house, going from room to room and inquiring about the children and their activities. It took her awhile to remember that our natural children had been out of the house for some time.

She spent several minutes staring at the appointment calendar that hung on the wall and continued asking a myriad of questions. She checked and rechecked her transcribing jobs, trying to see what had been done and what needed attention.

Then Susan sat down at the kitchen table and started telling me about an incredibly vivid dream experience that she was slowly beginning to recall. As her descriptions ensued, she explained that the images were beginning to fade in much the way that normal dreams often fade as we wake up and struggle to remember.

Susan was quite taken by the closeness and unity of the people and the vibrant colors, feathers, and many artful creations used in the ceremonies. She was particularly enamored by groupings of large drums that she remembered, beating in unison during long, slow processional dancing.

Apparently, she had traded places with the little Priestess. She was in the little one's body, or "dolly" as Sha Sha called it, in Mokhi Maya, just as the little one had alleged. Apparently, there was a series of ceremonies that was a part of her rites of passage as the priestess-in-training. There were large public gatherings and resplendent pageantry in which the next priestess was expected to be present, to participate in and be seen by the general populace.

Because of the trauma that the little one had suffered, she was excused by the Source from the inordinate stress of tedious processions and public exposure. As an almost "child-god" to her people, all eyes were upon her. There was a somewhat unreasonable burden that she be the absolute picture of decorum and perfection. This situation was brought about even more profoundly due to the events that led to the child's apparent death by her mother's hand, followed by her seemingly miraculous resurrection.

When Susan merged into the child's body (dolly) in Mokhi Maya, she was able to take on the countenance of the child and fulfill the requirements of the culture; thereby mitigating some of the excessive expectations that the child was being forced to endure.

Some days later, the child reemerged, all cuddly and full of giggles. Apparently she had just returned from an important banquet. Everyone was watching her while she ate. The little one explained that she spilled some food on her clothing and was so embarrassed that she started to cry. Then, the reigning Priestess and all in attendance spilled food on their clothing and everyone started laughing and hugging.

It was supposedly a very healing event, not only for the priestess-in-training, but for some much needed reality testing for her people as well. The Source called it a significant bonding experience and that the little Priestess should have no further trouble participating in her own ceremonies and public appearances.

As previously mentioned, the little Priestess was a real marvel at finding and selecting presents. She had a talent for finding just the thing that would inspire or validate a person's interests and private desires, often containing a spiritual theme. Sometimes the gifts would even be a bit prophetic, choosing something that you thought you really didn't need, only to discover that in a few days or weeks it was precisely what was required.

In her Mokhi Maya home she would get many, many presents. It was a tradition of the people to bring her gifts on special occasions or for no occasion at all. Sha Sha would explain that the gifts were not for her personally, but were to honor the divine light inside of her that came from the Source of the readings and the teachings. (She often giggled and blushed when she said such things.)

There were so many gifts that it became necessary to create a sort of warehouse or museum where all the treasures could be stored. Sometimes people would even bring finely crafted jewelry or toys made of gold. The child was not allowed to keep more than three gifts with her in her quarters at any one time.

One day, I was fully in the throes of unsettling, quiet terror while pondering how to stretch the family finances to sufficiently cover our burgeoning debt. The little one apparently heard my soulful lamentations and my quip that, "It sure would be good to be able to have a little Mokhi Maya gold to fulfill some of our financial obligations."

Sha Sha, while she was in Mokhi Maya and remembering my plight, told Labhar about her life in the future, where he was her Tati, who needed something called money that you could get with gold. So Labhar and his little sister snuck into the temple treasury and secured some gold objects that they decided to bury near a boulder. They reasoned that I could come and find it in my present life; thus having more money so Sha Sha could buy more presents. Apparently, it made quite a ruckus as the reigning Priestess had to intervene and clarify to whom the treasures belonged.

As Sha Sha was questioned, she was again told of how she lived in a strange place in the future with her brother who had become her Tati. There was supposedly much concern regarding this tall tale. It seemed somewhat implausible and incredulous. Again, there was concern that the child was losing her mind, suffering from the physical and emotional trauma that had been visited upon her by her rageful mother.

The High Priestess went into a deep meditation, not knowing what to do about this incredible story. Sha Sha explained that when her Priestess returned she was smiling and shaking her head. According to the little one, the Source had told the Priestess that Sha Sha's experiences were not a fantasy; every word was true.

After that, those in attendance would just listen to the stories of her many adventures in the land of the future. Some were a bit hard to believe, but all listened in awe and wonder, especially Labhar.

So apparently, this phenomena that had so been so extricably woven into the fabric of our life was found to be just as odd and thought provoking in Mokhi Maya as it was in this modern time.

Chapter 14

Jeb and Lissy

The Child Protective Services job required periodic out-of-town travel to visit what was termed Residential Child Care Facilities where juveniles had been placed by my agency. Some of our wards required specialized services that were difficult to provide locally; at other times there were simply no openings in nearby facilities for the kind of supervision and treatment that a child might require.

On occasion, I would have to go as far away as Denver to attend a staff meeting that would hopefully ensure that our taxpayers were getting what they were paying for; and with the child being adequately cared for and making progress within the guidelines of an individualized, court-ordered, treatment plan.

Just outside of Denver, near Golden, is a museum on top of a ridge named Outlook Mountain. The museum grew up around the final resting place of a legendary frontiersman and showman by the name of William Cody, also known as Buffalo Bill. I had always been drawn to the site but had never made the effort to actually stop and visit. During one excursion my inspection was completed early so I opted to spend some time at the museum and grave site before returning home.

At that time, it was an aging historic center that had not yet been remapped by the mindless mandates of political correctness. You could actually get a glimpse into how things were, as opposed to how someone believes they should have been.

As I strolled through the various western artifacts and exhibits, I began to feel a rather intense but peaceful energy that was slowly taking hold of me. It felt like a swirling mist, drawing me up and around a mountain peak.

I sat on a bench in a dimly lighted area as my skin began to tingle and the top of my head and hands started pulsing and feeling warm. Everything felt muted and far away. I began to feel the presence of some other spirit or being. At first it was not clear and was confusing to my conscious mind, as my thoughts struggled to understand and make sense of the sensations that were welling up inside me.

Then, I felt him. It was as though I was inside of another person. Initially, I could mostly feel his attitudes, his emotions. Soon, I could feel his body: rough, calloused hands; sunburned, wrinkled skin, and places in his body that were tight or aching. A tooth was bothering him, but he didn't pay much attention to it. He just ignored it. A sock was bunched up around a couple of toes in his right boot, but the toes were mostly just cold.

He was somewhere outside, staring into a campfire; he was cold, exhausted, feeling himself drifting somewhere, but not having a context to make sense it. He shrugged it off as just his imagination. You see, he was also aware of me looking in and communing with him.

There was some kind of motley colored cape or blanket pulled up tightly around his head and shoulders. He was hunched over holding a battered metal cup that had a chipped enamel coating. I presumed it held some kind of dark coffee; maybe it was a sort of bouillon or broth.

He was using the heat from the cup to warm his hands. As he sipped the bitter-tasting liquid it began to warm his body from the inside out. He felt old and tired, but very peaceful; content with himself. He was a bit of a loner. He was thinking to himself, "Beholdin' to none. Beholdin' to none."

I don't know how long I sat there. I remember a few museum visitors coming by; nodding and exchanging pleasantries, but I was mostly somewhere else. Later, I got up and began wandering around the exhibits again, but everything had shifted and changed.

The old saddles, buckskin clothing, boots and spurs, and firearms had somehow become more vibrant and alive. These were things that were familiar, the kind of things that you might actually own and use. It felt like I was looking into my own closet or tack room, rather than being some kind of a wandering observer in a museum.

The pictures felt more like a family album that would stimulate memories, rather than something impersonal and distant; not at all like amusements being offered to inquisitive voyeurs as entertainment.

It was getting late. I found a pay telephone and called home. I remember telling Susan that I was having a very profound experience and felt like I had been a thousand miles away and had been gone a hundred years. I didn't tell her anything else except I would be coming home soon.

Susan said, "I know. When you get home there will be some one here you will want to meet. She says her name is Lissy."

The house was dark and quiet, except for gentle music that was coming from Susan's office. I most likely dropped my bag at the usual spot, next to the kitchen table, and went to the refrigerator in quest for something to drink, probably a Diet Coke.

As I closed the door, I saw Susan peering at me from the other room. She was in the throes of yet another personality. She was smiling and approached cautiously, taking small steps, with her head tilted to one side and an inquisitive expression on her face.

"Sir, is that you? Your wife said you would be home soon. I do hope I am not intruding. These things just keep happening to me. I just don't know how I got here. I keep waking up in these strange places, but it is usually very interesting."

The words may not be exact, but that was pretty close. That is how she talked. Her name was Amaryllis, after the flower. Lissy was her nickname. She had a strong southern accent and was excruciatingly cordial and polite, at least until she got to know me better.

Like Sha Sha, she would giggle and laugh often. It turned out that she was a young girl of somewhere around twelve years of age. She was the daughter of a wealthy plantation owner outside of Asheville, North Carolina. She explained that she kept having these dreams in which she would be visiting other places.

Upon waking she would confide in her father, who seemed much more interested in her experiences than her mother. Her father apparently saw his child as having a wonderful imagination, whereas the mother was more concerned that people would find her "more than just a little peculiar."

After a couple of extended, but somewhat formal visits, the child looked at me and grabbed me by the arm in coquettish fashion. With great enthusiasm, she demanded to know why I kept playing these tricks on her. She called me Jeb and wanted to know what I was doing here in her dream. She had a delightfully curious nature and loved to ask questions on just about everything.

Once again, this was supposedly another lifetime of Susan. The Source allowed us to become acquainted and to learn from one another and would occasionally answer questions and fill in details that I had trouble figuring out on my own.

Apparently, Jeb was a fourteen-year-old from a neighboring plantation. It was much smaller and did not produce quite the lifestyle that Lissy's family enjoyed. However, Jeb was the closest "white playmate" in the area.

I had the impression that Jeb's father was a bit emotionally distant and always occupied with the daily affairs of running his plantation. He didn't have much room for frivolity. He may have been just some sort of overseer rather than the actual landowner. Jeb apparently visited often and was always teasing and playing tricks on Lissy.

These were the years leading up to the Civil War and I was not allowed to discuss the coming war as the Source had concerns that it could be unnecessarily traumatic for the child. She needed to enjoy her childhood. She did not need to know of the turmoil and devastation that would soon descend upon her home and community.

Lissy talked about her Daddy incessantly, which offered considerable insights into the times in which she lived. Sometimes I would question her, but once again the Source would tend to suspend conversation on subjects that might reveal information that neither of us should know; the reason being that these were things that needed to be lived and experienced and not tainted by predictive versions of what might be coming.

There were also choices to be made. It was the Source's preference that, in this particular case, we would not be unduly influenced by supposed understanding of possibilities that could have flowed between the current time and a lifetime in the mid- and latter 1800s.

Lissy's father was an abolitionist and was involved in the politics of international trade between the Americas and Europe. He was intimately involved in the growing rift between north and south and at times suffered public censure.

He had hoped for a boy, but Lissy was his only child. He contributed to Jeb's education and would sometimes take him on long trips so he could be exposed to larger cities and observe intricate business practices and political dealings. There were times when Lissy was a little jealous, but all in all, everything seemed to be in order.

Once, Hawk Woman appeared for a cameo comment. She wanted us to know how proud she was of Lissy; that she had a very wonderful life and accomplished much during that period.

Lissy became a playmate of the little priestess, much to her delight, but sometimes to her dismay. A bit of sibling rivalry would occasionally raise its head, but nothing inordinate. Again, it seemed that Lissy had "dreams" in which she regularly visited several places and this experience was just one of them. It took some time for Sha Sha to realize that she had become Lissy in a future lifetime. But she seemed mostly just happy to have a playmate that was also living in more than one world at a time.

Lissy was fascinated by automobiles and television. We once took her to the Grand Junction airport so she could see people getting on planes and flying off into the sky. She found it hard to believe that this was possible and questioned if this was another one of Jeb's tricks, "just to make me (her) feel foolish."

When she told her Daddy about airplanes, she came back expressing her father's concerns that her imagination might be getting a bit out of control. But, to his credit, he almost always gave her the benefit of a doubt, while cautioning that she might consider keeping it to herself because others might not be as understanding. In that regard, I guess things have not really changed all that much over the last one hundred and fifty years.

Lissy had some playmates in the slave quarters and would sometimes sneak off to participate in their religious services. Her mother was very concerned for her safety and reputation. Lissy had a nanny who would usually cover for these apparent lapses in judgment, which were generally sanctioned by the father.

During one of her most emotional visits, Lissy discovered black people on television being portrayed and accepted as a natural and equal part of the everyday life. She cried great tears of joy, witnessing that the dreams of her father and others would actually be realized. We went out to the mall just so she could find "an actual negro" and watch how they interacted in our modern world.

"Big Sister" (Sha Sha) once quipped in hushed tones, admonishing Lissy not to stare and grin at black people all the time, because it was impolite. Lissy seemed a little taken back, but upon reflection accepted the criticism.

Her father had supposedly made arrangements to try and leave a substantial portion of land to his freed slaves. Apparently, he was especially concerned about those families who had served his plantation from the previous generations. Although some had their own plots of land, he knew that the local culture and legal system would not support his efforts or honor the land deeds once he was gone.

So even though some of his workers had been freed, there was really nowhere for them to go; they were free only so long as they remained under his protection. He made plans to find a way to acquire land further out West, even as far away as Oregon, in the hope that communities could be started where black people could live in relative freedom and enjoy the fruits of their own labors; a right that continues to be challenged for free people even in these times.

Lissy's father was not the only one with these ideas, but he was one of the few of the ruling aristocracy that actually made attempts to put those ideas into action. Jeb had traveled with him in quest of guides and scouts who might know where to find suitable land out West for the proposed project.

Apparently, Lissy's uncle was furious with her father for attempting to give away much of the family heritage to "common slaves." As the war approached, Lissy was eventually sent to France for safety and to get an education in a young ladies' finishing school. Meanwhile, a substantial part of the family's wealth was moved to a northern state, Tennessee to be exact, where they (and the family's wealth) survived the war relatively intact.

Jeb continues to emerge, from time to time. Occasionally he will visit, looking out at the landscape, shaking his head, rolling over, and sort of going back to sleep. I have been allowed to see how he dressed and how he lived.

Once I waited with him for three days in a pine forest at the edge of open range, where he hoped for a rendeveous to receive supplies and some kind of "further instructions."

He was riding a chestnut-colored horse at the time. He was very fond of it. I think they went through the war together. Later I noticed that he had a dark-maned bay with three white stockings, along with a pack mule. We both remain fond of horses.

Once we were riding in a buggy of some sort. He was wearing a dark suit with a stiff gray-colored shirt. He was coming back from some kind of religious service. It may have been a wedding, but I don't think that Jeb himself ever found a long lasting relationship in that lifetime. His wandering lifestyle, more than likely, was too disruptive for anything permanent.

It took me almost ten years to finally recognize his full name, but it did seem to bring some closure to discover it and to know that he actually existed. No matter how profound the experience, I sometimes find doubts in my wandering mind, but they are mostly fleeting.

Jeb served as a Cavalry Scout. He was what some would term a spy for the Union. After the war with his home in ruins, like so many others, he drifted westward. He was strongly affected by the massive, brutal deaths and casualties of the several conflicts in which he was a witnessing participant.

He reached deep inside and was able to do some esoteric work, helping discarnate souls of mutilated and traumatized soldiers move on, away from the battlefields and into their next phase of existence.

While still young, he had traveled with Lissy's father to Florida, where both escaped and freed slaves had mingled with the Native American peoples. Jeb was allowed to attend ceremonies and became very enamored of some of their shaman-istic practices and teachings. Though he had been a devout Bible-reading churchgoer, this experience helped him to better deal with some of the esoteric experiences that he later encountered.

There was much he was never able to figure out or resolve within his own mind. At some point he just accepted the occasional otherworldly experience as something that would take care of itself, figuring it was simply beyond his need to understand. Sometimes I wish I could have better retained that wisdom.

He spent some time up north, in New York City to be exact. He even authored a bit of a book, which gave him some fleeting credentials and contacts that served as a catalyst for some government-sponsored excursions out West. Someday, perhaps the universe will bring me a copy of it. That could be very revealing, at least from the standpoint of my own personal edification. It might put some of our remaining prurient questioning to rest.

Eventually, Jeb became a resource for the government and was involved in a series of expeditions, including surveying and establishing relationships with Indians, sometimes as a civilian Scout. He once traveled with Gibson in what became known as Yellowstone National Park. He was briefly consulted about, though not present in the events around Custer and the Little Big Horn in Montana. He spent some time northwest of Cheyenne and participated in a surveying expedition in the Estes Park area in Colorado. He also spent time in portions of New Mexico and Arizona.

Jeb was betrayed by those more interested in glory than in attempting to find more equitable and peaceful solutions to "the Indian problem." The war and these associations made him even more distrustful of governments.

He was once portrayed as a traitor and renegade, being ostracized by those he had once served. He never saw Lissy again, but he lived a wondrous and charmed life as one of the many unnoticed western explorers and pioneers of that age. He lived his life his way, "Beholdin' to none," and died of fever in the wilderness near a remote outpost.

Briefly, he found one who truly loved and understood him, but they became separated. They always remembered, but never found each other again. He still dreams of her, sometimes he can feel her presence as they reach out to each other, still searching, through time and space.

It seems to me that Lissy's emergence was a result of my rather unsettling encounter and resurrection of Jeb. Lissy's presence, somehow orchestrated by what we called the Source, offered me a deeper and more profound opportunity to discover, augment, and explore from within another side of human consciousness.

This process was more than an interesting concept or observation. It is a direct multidimensional experience, where memory becomes flesh.

I think the primary purpose for this partial emergence of Jeb was to enable me to better comprehend—with empathy, through my own direct experience—the path that my beloved Susan was walking. It also helped Jeb to sort out some things that he had always wondered about. It gives him a chance to complete a few things that he felt were left undone.

Lissy was not with us for long. Her presence only lasted a few months. But it provided an interesting perspective into that which the Source referred to as "what the channels were simultaneously experiencing on several levels."

Chapter 15

Hathrell's Mission

O ne day in the summer of 2000, I was pushing myself particularly hard while exercising. With eyes closed, I was sprinting across my treadmill, gasping toward a goal of getting the machine to register a distance of two miles before 24 minutes had elapsed. This would be a considerable accomplishment, since I had rather seriously weakened my ankles a couple of years before by falling out of a tree.

At one point, I even questioned if I would ever be able to do much hiking again, but now I was clearly on the mend. Along with my own efforts, and the diet and exercise recommendations of the Source, I was getting my strength and endurance back.

As I stomped along I began to clearly see, in my mind's eye, an exquisitely matured gentleman standing right in front of me. He was casually leaning up against the wall, gazing out the window with a sort of stoic expression. He was very Nordic looking. He had snow-white hair, which came almost to his shoulders, and sported a well-manicured full beard.

His skin had an almost translucent quality with absolutely no blemishes of any kind. There was a quiet stillness and an almost penetrating radiance that emanated from the figure.

He turned to look at me with the bluest eyes that you will ever see. He was fit and muscular and wore white clothing that was simple yet elegant. When our eyes met he gave a slight nod with a hint of a smile. I surmised that he was somehow pleased that I had discovered him.

I opened my eyes, shook off his image, looked at the gauge on the treadmill, as I gasped for my last few breaths and admitted defeat. For now, two miles at 24 minutes was still well beyond my grasp. As I cooled down, I wrapped myself in an old gray army blanket and sat on my sheepskin preparing to meditate. I briefly saw him again in my mind's eye and wondered about what I had encountered.

His form seemed quite familiar. I had the impression that I had seen him before, but could not remember where. I recalled some teachings which claimed that in the astral world the visage of angels would often appear to be perfect and without blemish. With my usual doubts, I once again wondered if this was just my imagination, or if it was something that had been induced by a shortage of oxygen during my desperate jog to nowhere.

Susan was again taking a break from finger pounding on her computer and suggested we go out to lunch. That was fine with me; I was a bit weary of resuming my work on a montage of case management reports and evaluations. At the time, I had a contract with the Department of Veteran's Affairs for disabled veterans as a sort of itinerate case manager and vocational evaluator.

We went to the 7th Street Café which had recently moved to the Main Street location where a Café called Jitters had previously resided. It is a location close to the post office; a good place to eat while we were out on errands. The little one liked to have her "Mati Susan" read and explain the jokes and riddles that were found in the little monthly newsletter that is placed on each booth and table.

After glancing at the familiar menu and ordering, Susan said the Source wanted to know if I had something to tell them. I thought a moment, but could think of nothing. Then, I remembered the intra-psychic encounter with the Nordic-looking apparition. It was a real "dreaming while awake" experience.

I began to describe him when Susan said, "Well, I see you have met Hathrell." She said this, pointing upward with her index finger. This had become a signal to help me confirm that what was being said was coming from the Source. The Source expressed its approval and satisfaction that I was able to make this connection without the requirement of meeting him through the channel, but rather as a direct experience, within my own consciousness. I most likely rolled my eyes like an annoyed teenager, as I was beginning to hear this theme much too often.

So many times this Source had encouraged me to learn to awaken my own abilities and not to always rely on the abilities of Susan or the little priestess. I was always being told, "The Christ is always available to meet you within your own temple if you will but allow it."

Well, I really had not much of a clue as to how to do that, and besides Susan was the real channel, so why not at least attempt to make good use of what was obviously at hand? I had heard this prattle so often that it had become a bit of a cliché and, I must confess, a bit tiresome. My occasional psychic and intuitive glimpses were not even close to what Susan had been experiencing and manifesting on an almost daily basis for many years.

Nevertheless, I listened and re-listened to the repetitious reminders. Put simply, they repeatedly explained that someday I might be required to "do my own work" and the experience with the Source should be looked upon as part of "an apprenticeship in which both channels were to learn and to accomplish."

It was explained that this Hathrell had been with us for some time now and that he had come "to help us with the next step of the transition that has already begun." He was introduced as an angel of the highest order. My sense was that he was sort of a figurehead, a conglomerate of consciousness if you will, representing several angelic or spirit beings.

Hathrell, an additional presence with his own voice and mannerisms, emerged through Susan and confirmed this "introduction." I again noted that he seemed pleased that I was able to receive this impression. It was also explained that as a member of the angelic hosts he could manifest in any form that was desired and that if I thought about it I might realize that I had indeed seen him several times before, even in the physical world.

Hathrell remained a sort of always present, but predominately in the background, force that also resorted to the "peek-a-boo" format. Every so often he would check in just to let us (me) know he was still around. Like Hawk Woman, he would sometimes have a comment or two. He appeared to be humble and unassuming and occasionally exhibited a sort of "tongue-in-cheek" sense of humor. I had the sense that he was downright fascinated at being able to have this direct and interactive encounter with the human condition in the twenty-first century.

Though he was obviously capable of occupying Susan's body much like one of her own soul personalities, it was explained that this was a completely separate phenomenon. He was to be considered as both a guardian and guide along the way, again as a manifestation of the angelic realm.

One day while Susan was driving in traffic, the car suddenly swerved from the right to the left lane. The driver in the car behind us suddenly locked his brakes and slid screeching right up beside us. In the other car was a shaken driver with a sheepish grin mouthing an apology. Susan gasped and looked as if she had become briefly disoriented. Then, she recounted how the steering wheel felt like it had been wrenched from her hands, abruptly angling the car into the next lane.

It was explained that Hathrell had made the successful intervention, thus avoiding what could have been a very serious rear-end collision. Hathrell apologized for the jerky, abrupt movement, but explained that the physical flesh bodies are so dense that it was sometimes hard for him to move smoothly. Apparently, he had needed to act quickly, and his actions were not as coordinated as he would have liked. Whatever had happened, we were grateful to have avoided a potentially serious accident.

The Source assured us, once again, that all was in order. I was once again encouraged to continue to trust in the guidance and intervention that was being provided. It appeared that I was always needing reassurance. It was suggested that we should consider ourselves to be "living in a state of grace during the coming transition."

As the months came and went, it did become more and more apparent that some kind of shift was taking place. It was becoming harder and harder for me to tell if the Priestess were mimicking Susan or if Susan were mimicking the Priestess. The Source explained that what I was observing was part of the process of re-integration. I was told the process might not be what I was expecting, and that it could become very emotional. Once again, there were assurances that all was well, just as it was meant to be. I was told that there were things that I didn't need or want to know.

Perhaps this is a good time to discuss what was happening to time during these various visitations. We were told that although we experience time as a linear thing, in actuality time is what we might call circular. This discussion had become a major theme during the last few months.

Sha Sha would come and leave at various ages during her lifetime. To her, everything was all in a progressive order. But here, in our present life, it was a bit of a jumble. She came older, then younger; then younger and older at the same time; and sometimes even as an infant. The same was not so true of Hawk Woman.

However, after a while this aberration in time seemed to be quite normal and actually was not so hard to track, at least most of the time. I began to look at it as if there were this whole lifetime, or series of life experiences, in which various parts would haphazardly pop out due to a particular need for expression or attention that related to situations and events of the present time.

I sort of envisioned it like a chiropractic adjustment. Your spine goes from the top to the bottom, or if you wish from the bottom to the top. If there is a problem or strain in your thoracic (middle back) area it might be helpful to get an adjustment, either through natural day-to-day movement or with a physician's intervention.

However, an adjustment to the thoracic area could result in a change in a little different angle in your lower back or neck. So you might then seek an adjustment to a cervical (neck) or lumbar (lower back) area. But, then that can again impact how the thoracic area is aligned.

So, it can be a system where you keep working on what needs attention and watch the ripple effect all up and down the line.

To me this is what was happening in Sha Sha's life; different parts would "pop out" at different times needing communion and attention. I suspect that is also how it works regarding which personality might emerge at which time. This is also influenced by what circumstances are present in the current life and how those events might be correlated or coordinated, so there is communication and impact to both times and places.

Another way I have looked at it is as a hula hoop that keeps spinning around. There may be some kinks in it here and there.

It is not round. It wobbles. As you straighten out the various kinks, the hoop becomes more precise; more round if you will, more perfected with less wobble. But in the weakened areas, the kinks may continue to show up from time to time and may respond to some additional corrective interaction as other corrected points on the circle also come into play.

And it seemed to make perfect sense to me that sometimes the kink being worked on would be triggered by what Susan would be going through in this life—in the form of a person or a place challenging situation. It would seem that wisdom and experience from or by another era and personality could also be used to address Suzy's particular need or kink; thus simultaneously making her more able to address the other times and places where help might be needed.

I see it all as an interactive thing, all happening right now, through all the times and ages. And this must be correct, for after all, the Source tells me I am correct! Of course, that all depends on whether or not this "Source" is correct in what it is saying and doing.

Based on the track record, it was not perfect, but seemed to be doing a fairly good job. Perhaps the manifestation of this "Source" is also a work in progress and improves or becomes more precise along with the progression of time (that allegedly does not exist) and experience (which has supposedly already happened).

Apparently, human comprehension can only go so far. Thus is the nature of these things which cannot be fully understood while the soul inhabits the current limitations of the earthly dimension.

So Hathrell nods with confirmation, and Jeb shakes his head in amusement. Such is the nature of these strange goings on. It seems there are some things which are simply beyond our human capacities. Sometimes it is best, and certainly easier, to simply tell the story and trust whatever meaning there might be to another time and place when clearer comprehension of such things might be possible.

And in unison they say "YES!!!"

Until this time, I have avoided discussion of the dark side of the Priestess, in order to build sufficient background and insight to make it easier to grasp what was being accomplished.

There was an angry, tortured, vindictive priestess that had emerged from the childhood cauldron of betrayal, torture, and disillusionment. She was very adept, powerful, relentless, and unyielding. By her mere presence she could sometimes command others to do her bidding, even unto their own destruction. She could become replete with a seething, unquenchable rage that could fuel an endless campaign of vindictiveness.

She could glare into your eyes and leave you helpless to do anything but follow her will, metaphorically and sometimes literally. This was as the "dark side" of her force. This was how she could have become and, in fact, may have become in that time and culture that the little one referred to as Mokhi Maya.

If this were left unchecked, she could have brought war, famine, and pestilence to her people in an ever growing, but never satiated bid for power, control, and revenge. Through her mother, the dark forces had attacked the very heart of the evolving society that was intended to be based on the resurrection of the ancient teachings and sacred truths. With the powers of their priestess turned to the dark side, seeds could be sown that could render an entire people and heritage into utter abandonment and desolation.

In this place, this current era, she could release her rage at a radio or computer and literally reduce it to static. She could coerce a waiter or waitress to put her at the head of the line and demand superior service. She could bolt from a car and march through the desert with utter contempt and outrage coursing through her entire being, until physical exhaustion would bring her back home and back into balance.

During one dark phase, she became so brimming with rage she grabbed a broom and pounded it against the garage door, producing serveral holes. It was the most violent thing I had ever seen her do.

Moments later, Susan emerged, stating, "Did I do that? I don't know what got into me." During the next few days she would return to the door and stared at the damage over and over again. In that one relatively small act, her trauma had been forever revealed unto herself.

In her darkness, Sho Adh Shahannah might have been easily provoked, instantly giving into an unquenchable rage. However, when she was well monitored, she (and we) learned to understand, redirect, and release these powerful side effects of betrayal.

As Sha Sha resolved her conflicts, the trauma was reduced, her abilities increased and she became more balanced, focused, and empowered to be a channel of blessings. She flourished, and the dark side lost the potential for power over her. As she released her guilt and despair she was no longer vulnerable to the dark forces.

It was as a revelation from one part of her to the rest of her. Though it had remained hidden for twenty-thousand years, maybe longer, it became the beginning of the final unraveling of a scar that had been inflicted at the inception—the first incarnation of a virgin soul (Hawk Woman) cast into the earthly experience. This was a final emotional outburst, a final episode that the Source had cautiously foreshadowed.

Now there had been a turning point of conscious revelation, an opening of an ancient boil of putrid, festering infection, from deep within the depths of her soul. It was another beginning, a pivotal revealing to herself of the result of the trauma of what a child priestess was forced to endure. "It did not *have* to have been; yet was entered into at the soul's own discretion for her own crucifixion and potential for resurrection."

Here then, was a shift in the balance: the culmination of a returning of an unquenchable peace to a great soul, gravely injured but now in the throes of grace-filled healing.

Simply put, Hathrell had been summoned to help keep things under control and to make smooth a potentially difficult transition; to grab the wheel of the vehicle from time to time; and to stave off accidents so that, through grace, things never got out of control.

Our little priestess, while in her coma in Mokhi Maya, had been united with her big brother, Labhar, within another time and place where a whole lifetime could be devoted to softening, comforting and revealing the atrocities that had been wrought upon the child priestess.

She had come to a place of support and comfort to buffer the maddening assaults upon her innocence and dignity so that an even stronger and more worthy priestess could arise with compassion, forgiveness, and healing; just like the rising of the fabled Phoenix bird from its own ashes.

Now was coming her time of awakening. This is what the whole experience was about: an intensive slow-motion time out, in another time and place where this soul's personality could absorb, react, and recover from the trauma of her abusive mother. Then she could be gently reinserted into her time and place; that she might serve her people with clarity and purity of purpose; that her people might flourish and grow in the harmony and righteousness that the Source had intended.

The priestess did not emerge from some mythological or metaphorical dream time. It was the other way around. To her, this modern day American existence is the dream land. We were her "Alice in Wonderland," experience; her journey down the yellow brick road to the "Wizard of Oz." Though this perspective may not correlate with precision, it can perhaps add to the understanding of those here, in the attempt to grasp this intra-psychic reality of this phenomenon.

Hathrell was here to hold our hands and be our steadfast guardian. He is an aspect of the Source, formed by God, and sent as a more directly responsive, angelic being, compatible with the essential needs and understandings of the entities involved.

The Source was hinting that the end of this process was near. "They" continued to use words like reintegration. The signs that I could see were vague, but becoming clearer. I was beginning to have hope that my beloved might be returned to me once more.

Almost twenty years ago, I had asked the Source how long would be this process, this presence of the little priestess that called herself Sha Sha, the Priestess of Mokhi Maya. I was told it would be "soon," that the time would pass more quickly than I could imagine; though it would be challenging at times, there would be much that could be gained from this experience that was being "allowed" to happen.

We had missed a lifetime of the more personal intimacies between a man and a woman. In truth, we had become more of a brother and sister than a husband and wife; an understood side effect of the daily presence of so many personages. Our relationship came to reflect more of what we had apparently been in the previous existences, rather than what we may have appeared to be in this one.

Susan occasionally stated that she never really had a life because of the needs of the little ones that lived within her. When the Priestess was present, it often felt more like I was a single parent than a husband. Yet, the child was also a cherished member of my life and as real as anyone I had ever met. And, once again, Grandfather-mother Source was ever present.

All these personages were evolving into this single priestess that Susan and I called "Big Sister." At times she had a heavy, sorrowful heart; yet she was full of such compassion and resolve.

There was such a sense of dignity and clarity of wisdom about her, and her sense of humor was second to none.

Reflecting over what I had witnessed during the last two decades just left me in a state of awe and wonder.

Though time had taken its toll, perhaps now would come our time: a time for Susan and I to be together once more. I knew something was coming, but was not sure what. I re-read some books and articles about how multiple personalities sometimes reintegrate. Some things made sense and were similar and familiar. But much of the so-called "professional" information was woefully inadequate. It was still obvious to me that this process is not something that could be simply orchestrated, but could only be partially observed with rather limited support and occasional participation.

Susan began busying herself with things around the house. There were special efforts at cleaning and rearranging things that had not been touched for years. Closets were gone through, boxes were opened as she sorted out a wardrobe that had been collected over three decades. She commented that she would not be needing these anymore, but it was good to go though them once again. I suggested that maybe it was time for a Goodwill donation. She quipped, "This could be done later, but now is not the time."

She said she wanted to do something with the living room and wanted to add some accents. I suggested that it would be good to have some things with dark blue in them. She quipped, "Then this is what we shall get for you."

Then she decided that we should get some new living room furniture. I was a bit reluctant, once again being concerned about the expense. She began some rather expert negotiation, stating we should get something that I would be comfortable with and would last me the rest of my life.

We had not always agreed on how to decorate our houses. However, over the years I must admit that if it had been left up to me we would most likely be sitting on orange crates. Susan's theatre and costuming experience brought out her artistic side and again, I had to admit; though reluctantly, that I usually liked what she put together. However, she had never seemed so attentive to what it was that I might like to have. I kept looking for "the catch" but somehow didn't find any.

I suggested that, if we were going to spend some money, we might first make sure our computers were up to date as it was obvious that it was once again time to consider upgrading. She agreed that it was something I should consider, but felt that her particular "byte machines" were quite adequate for the time being and would not need to be replaced.

So hand-in-hand we toured the furniture stores and I finally got that big, man-sized leather chair that I had always wanted, along with a manly looking sofa to match. I had wanted to buy some bookcases and rearrange our library section. The Priestess emerged and started to question my arrangement; but Susan, sounding firm and in charge, responded that "Tati should have things arranged the way that he likes."

If this was going to be the new attitude around the house, I liked it.

We began to review our finances. I started to put together an interim plan that might hopefully make it possible for us to have some semi-retired years. To my surprise, she agreed with most of my market observations and plans that I had posited regarding real estate. Both the Source and Susan agreed that it would be good for me to use my own judgment, move cautiously, but steadfastly to implement my investment plan. This was a bit surprising because, although Susan had always been supportive in the abstract, she was usually a bit hesitant to see me actually start putting real estate deals together. The Source cautioned me not to buy certain kinds of real estate in certain places.

At times during our marriage, we had been heavily in debt and really struggled. Finally, it appeared that things might start coming together, but it was also important that we would start making our assets work for us and grow; rather than being stagnant or hemorrhaging, as too often had been the case. So before long, we had two new rentals that were adequately leveraged for a good return; but we also had a little positive cash flow. I was constantly on the prowl for even more careful investments.

Susan suggested that we take a close look at our life insurance needs. She said, "Well, just consider what would happen if we were to lose one of our incomes." I asked if this was a suggestion from the Source. She said it was to be my decision, but I might consider it.

It made no sense to me. I had spent a lot of money on life insurance over the years that I had never needed. It was good to have when we were vulnerable, with a young family and all. But now the house was paid off, and for the first time there seemed to be cash to spare. As we were aging, premiums were becoming quite expensive. I would prefer to put more into real estate rather than to feed the negativity. I reasoned that, if we had the Source in our corner, things would always work out. Often we were told that financially we would have what was needed, though not always what we may have wanted. So why waste money on insurance when you could invest it?

I sought out a new accountant familiar with real estate. We even reviewed some estate planning and updated our wills. Susan, who usually did not spend much time attending to family finances, insisted she come along to meet our new CPA. After the session, she touched my arm and raised her index finger, confirming the Source's presence. I was told that I would be in good hands with this particular person; he was very thorough, knowledgeable, and had commendable integrity.

Yes, it seemed we were finally going to get through this endless transition that the Source had been relentlessly describing over the years. The children were grown, out of the house, getting on with their own lives. Susan was ever more present.

We were beginning to have long walks and endless conversations with just the two of us about everything and nothing. We were reminiscing about our life together; how we met; the little Oakmont trailer that was our first home; how Mollie had come to live with us and eventually succumbed to Alzhiemer's disease; and dozens of other things; but basically, through it all, how we had somehow pulled together and made things work.

When we looked into each other's eyes I could still see my sophisticated New Yorker, designing her costumes; full of passion and enthusiasm for everything Cayce and the coming new age in which we were all to participate.

She could still see that straight-spined, young buck sergeant, an air-cavalry trooper from Fort Hood, with all the confidence and promise that only youth can offer.

We had it all, and everything in between; including all the psychic encounters and pilgrimages we had made. Yes, we had been on a marvelous adventure and raised two fine children.

As we sat in the café on Main Street, the Source indicated how pleased they had been with our progress. It was suggested that the diet that had been recommended would actually "serve the entity well for the rest of the lifetime, though there will almost always be some challenge with the weight."

Looking to the future, the Source began reviewing the next life stages with us and added that, if I ever had to bring my aging mother to Grand Junction from her home in Arizona, I should fly and not attempt to drive her by automobile.

The next few days seemed rather hectic. Susan was charging around with so many projects. I kidnapped her and took her up to my special place, high above the city on the mesa in the Colorado National Monument. It was a place we had often visited when we still lived in Telluride and just before we made our decision to come to Grand Junction.

On the way back, Susan pulled the car off to the side of the road and put her hand on my arm. There was a particular song playing on the radio. She said the Source had bid her to stop and point it out so that I might "listen and hear."

It was a country and western tune with a theme that had something to do with sailing your ship until the river runs dry. Over the last couple of years Susan had become quite fond of listening to country and western music on the radio. She said she liked it because it often speaks from the heart and tells of life's challenges and joys, with family, couples, and friends.

We hadn't heard from our son for a few days so she made a call and told him how proud she was of him and then bid him good-bye. Our daughter had called a few days before. Yes, it is good to have children who are people you are proud to know.

Our Priestess had been peering out from time to time, but seemed to have something on her mind that was troubling her. A few days prior the Source again announced that very soon my Priestess would be returning to Mokhi Maya.

Hathrell once again explained that it would be very emotional, but that they would be with us. He cautioned me to expect it and prepare for it.

I no longer remember the order of things but I remember an incident in which a slightly indignant priestess stomped right up to me, demanding to know if I knew that her "Dollies fell down." I wasn't sure what she meant, but she kept asking over and over, with a slight accusation in her voice.

I took her by the hand and we went into the bedroom. On a top shelf was a display of twelve or fifteen dolls. These had been collected over the years as gifts. Susan had recently organized them so that they could be displayed as a collection. Sometimes a doll would come down for the little one to enjoy. Some of them did not stand up very well and would fall over. So we looked. I assured her that they were all still standing. She looked at me with a rather confused expression and disappeared back into the psyche of my beloved.

One evening while at the computer, I felt a tap on my shoulder. It was Sha Sha; I had not seen her for some time. Lately, she had usually emerged as her older manifestation that we always referred to as Big Sister.

Sha Sha was very solemn and presented me with a present. It was a petite little figurine that had been purchased during the previous Christmas. It was of a Native American Indian design. There was a mother with two young daughters sitting on her lap. The Priestess saw this as representing her Mati Susan, herself, and Big Sister.

She set it on the desk before me and said in her quiet little voice, "Here Tati, I want you to have this so you won't forget me." I gave her a quick hug that seemed to brighten her up a bit. In a preoccupied manner I returned to my computer screen.

Susan reemerged and asked what was wrong. Then, as if listening to the voices of her internal dialogue said, "Oh, I see. I understand."

I had a lot of plans for our new life together. A few years before, I had discovered that my grandmother had kept a Bible that belonged to my great-grandfather. Inside on a cover page, he had carefully recorded the births of four generations of our family. From this I discovered and began to resurrect my Scottish heritage.

We were attending the annual Scottish/Celtic festival in Grand Junction and had put together enough paraphernalia to offer a booth representing our family name and my newly obtained affiliation with our ancestral clan in Scotland.

We were having a great time. My son was also becoming involved. We were both learning the proper way to wear a Scottish kilt. I had even purchased a wee practice chanter and began to dream of being able to play bagpipes!

Susan seemed particularly attentive; she brought me good things to eat, gave me a back rub; told me that, despite all the obvious intrusions, she was happy with her life, and how proud she had been to be my wife. She said that she knew that things had been difficult for me, and she appreciated all that I had been through on her behalf.

She said the Source wanted me to know that my body was basically healthy; but I must, must, must, pay better attention to the diet. Then, it was suggested I try contacting an orthodontist familiar with progressive plastic retainers. It was suggested I use the "computer-net" to become better informed.

A little later Susan returned with a hand-crafted reproduction of a Scottish targe, a small battle shield, which was offered at a silent auction. She said I would need to have a good shield and she wanted me to have it. Sparing no expense, she bid up the price until we were able to claim it.

Then, with the full presence of her Source she turned toward the northeast and gazed toward the heavens. She put her hands together in a familiar mudra. I very clearly remember her saying ...

"Next year you should go to Estes Park and attend the festival there. It will be of great benefit for you. For there, you may very well find the portal to the next phase of your life."

That was good news to my ears. Susan was somewhat less enamored by Scottish heritage than I. I was hoping to travel to other Celtic festivals, but she always seemed a little resistant, saying she had too much to do. Now, I had an actual mandate from the Source! Yes, that was especially good to hear!

Later that evening, Susan was resting in the master bedroom while I was going through the mail, doing some filing and paying bills. There was a growing pile of books that I was sporadically reading. I was sorting them out; putting them back on shelves.

I began to sense a very ominous presence.

Everything grew profoundly quiet and still. It seemed to stop me in mid-motion and left me suspended and tingling. After a few moments, I instinctively climbed up the stairs, entered the meditation room, sat down, pulled the old woolen military blanket around me, and lit the candle.

It was as if I were being wrapped in a protective shroud while all thought was suspended. There was a sense of heavy, mournful compassion. It was very serene and lingered for well over an hour. I had only experienced such an event one or two other times in my life. I was inwardly aware that Susan was also experiencing this energy.

She called to me and asked me to come to bed. Hathrell stirred and reminded me that we had been told that the little one would be moving on very soon. Once again, like a repeated mantra, I was told I should expect it and prepare for it the best I could.

We drifted off to sleep entwined in each other's arms.

Chapter 16

Saying Good-Bye

The morning after the Scottish festival we were up early and busy with plans for the day. Susan put on a jacket that had been one of the little one's favorite sets of "priestess clothes," as she called them. The outfit consisted of a loose fitting jacket with matching slacks. There was an interesting pattern with several bright colors. Here and there were some bold mystical symbols that were mostly of an American Indian design.

I remember her hurriedly combing her long, flowing hair. Once again, she had misplaced her brush, so she was using mine. I never knew for sure if Susan actually liked her hair that way or just let it grow long because she knew it pleased me. Either way, over the years, it had simply become a part of Sha Sha's identity. She went to her jewelry box and took longer than usual to pick out a necklace. She tried on several, then insisted that she wanted me to decide. I selected what I knew had been one of her favorites.

Years before, she had been admiring it while we were strolling through a mall in Phoenix. Without asking, I simply bought it for her. It wasn't particularly expensive, but it was a bit more intricate than what she usually wore. We had both been attracted to the interesting patterns that were worked into the bronze-colored metal. With the beads, it was a bit suggestive of a Tibetan rosary, but more ornate. In my mind, it seemed to match the outfit.

I recall her exclaiming, "Perfect, just help me get in on!" There had been a problem with the clasp, which had been repaired more than once. As she gathered up and held her hair to one side, I placed the necklace around her neck and fastened it. She swung around and gave me an unusually strong hug and I kissed her on her forehead.

That morning we had an appointment with some folks to help us with our trees. A few were becoming brittle and infested with destructive insects. Our two acres of paradise were becoming overgrown and there was concern that a windstorm could bring some large limbs crashing down on the house. We had already had some damage done to our car.

Susan said she needed to do some errands. We agreed that I would stay home and wait for the arrival of the tree people. Susan was to return in a couple of hours so we could have a late breakfast at our favorite café on Main Street.

She was having trouble with her back. So, just as she had done so many, many times before, she laid face down on the carpet with her hands over her head. This was the signal for me to give her a quick massage and attempt an adjustment to her upper back.

A series of crisp pops and crunches erupted from her spine and she released her accompanying blissful sigh. Again she said it was "perfect." I guess perfect was her word for the day. She jumped up and gave me another long, lingering hug. She avoided eye contact and seemed to have something on her mind. She hesitated, then I very clearly remember her saying,

"Well, I think it is time for me to go now. Hopefully, I won't be gone too long. I'll be back before you know it." She stiffened a little and Hathrell emerged.

He paced back and forth a couple of times and told me to take care of myself and to know that I would always have his blessing and that the Source was always with me. It was typical Hathrell speak.

Susan bounced out of the house with the enthusiasm of a teenager on the way to a Friday night date and never looked back. She jumped into her white Honda Civic and sped down the five hundred feet of our driveway with gravel flying in all directions and dust boiling up into the air.

I wondered if it might be the heavy foot of Hathrell, as he never quite mastered the fine motor coordination required to smoothly operate a motor vehicle. He claimed he was keeping us safe. He had proven that, but I also wondered if maybe he just liked to drive.

The tree people came and left. I sat beneath the two gigantic weeping willow trees where we had conducted a ceremony to celebrate our twenty-fifth wedding anniversary. Susan had been instructed to commission a jeweler to create a set of wedding rings to commemorate the event. They were one-of-a-kind creations made out of silver.

Each ring had a stylized version of our own personal symbols that had been a part of the teachings that we had received over the years. Susan, of course, had an affinity with the Hawk. I had always had a bit of a fascination with the mountain lion or cougar as it is sometimes called. Of course, down in Mokhi Maya, they are cousins to the jaguar.

Blended into the rings was also the suggestive outline of the Phoenix, that mythological bird that would rise again from the fiery ashes of its destruction, becoming an even more beautiful version of its former self. Susan's ring included a small amethyst. It was a familiar gem. It was also a reflection of some of the teachings that the Source had shared when we still lived in Tucson.

It seemed to be an appropriate gift, yet the circumstances were a bit odd. I was told that we should not wear the rings, but I should keep them in a safe place for a future time when the symbology would become more apparent.

The metaphor of the Phoenix was mentioned more than once—so as to be sure I clearly saw it, and would remember its significance at some later date. The oddest part was when I was told that I would not remember the rest of what was being instructed until the time was right.

I was sitting in tall grass, with my back against one of the trees. In my hands I held my practice chanter, the instrument that is used for learning to play highland bagpipes and for working up new tunes. It seemed a good time to do some practicing. The little rosewood chanter was gripped tightly between my clumsy fingers. Hughy, my Scottish-born piping teacher, had been accusing me of gripping my chanter like a vulture desperately clutching a branch.

He is a grand old gentleman with much charisma and a great sense of humor. I was fortunate to have found him. He had told me that it was about time for me to consider ordering my pipes. However, I still needed just a little more time on the practice chanter before I was ready for that next step of tackling "the big pipes."

I was able to clumsily execute most of my doublings, as they are called. A couple of throws had been mastered and I was even making a good effort at asaulting a burl. So far, I had only been introduced to two tunes. So I played them over and over again; slowly, precisely, one note at a time; trying to follow my teacher's instructions.

So there I sat; first playing "Amazing Grace" for a while, then switching to "Just as I Am." I played and played; waited and waited. Susan was late. And a little later, she was still late.

I began to get more than a little annoyed. We only had one cell phone. I reasoned that she could at least call me, if something had come up or her plans had changed. As I continued playing, I gripped the chanter tighter and tighter, making it more and more difficult to play.

I wondered out loud if it might be possible for that vulture to get splinters in his feet. I paced around the two trees for a few minutes, then got into my vehicle. I reasoned that there was probably a good reason why she was late, but I needed to get on with my day for I too had things to accomplish!

As I drove down the driveway and turned onto the highway I began to feel those same ominous feelings that I had felt the night before. It was not anywhere nearly as strong. It might best be described as an aftershock. As I sped down the road, I remember being drawn to the newly opened Go-Fer convenience store, situated at the entrance to the Safeway store parking lot. I resisted before yielding to a compulsion to turn into the little strip mall.

I was hypnotically drawn behind the convenience store, where I drove my car, making an abrupt stop. Sitting in the middle of the lane was a little white car. It looked familiar. I got out. I looked inside. Susan's jacket and shoes were lying in the backseat. It was her car. But why did she leave it there?

Susan could be downright critical if someone didn't park perfectly between the painted lines. She always parked carefully. But her car wasn't even in a space. She always locked her car. Now it was unlocked with the window rolled down.

I stood there for a moment, with my door open and engine running, before noticing a young woman in a cashier's uniform rushing over to me. She looked anxious.

Stuttering, she asked me if I knew the person who owned the car. I said it was my wife's car. She told me that she had seen the lady drive up, stop the car, open the door, and collapse onto the blacktop. She explained that an ambulance had been summoned and took her away.

From my previous employment I was very familiar with the St. Mary's Emergency Room. I strode in, asking the receptionist if she had received a patient named Susan, a slightly obese lady of 54 years. She didn't answer, but fumbled with some papers. She asked me to sit down and said she would be right back.

Another lady appeared, escorting a man in a poorly fitting suit with a crooked tie. He walked right up to me and asked to see my identification. They guided me to a small waiting room, shut the door, and asked me to sit down.

They told me they did all they could, but Susan had passed away. It was a death notification. Over the years, I had conducted a number of these myself.

It all seemed like some hazy dream. I answered several questions, and I asked if I could see her. They looked at each other, asked me to sign some papers and said, "Of course."

The lady took me by the arm and walked me to another room where Susan was lying on a gurney, covered by a white sheet. I asked to be alone with her for awhile.

I sat and stared for the longest time. She was pasty white. I was most likely, perhaps obviously, in shock. She was not breathing, but her skin was still warm and supple. I kept waiting for her to wake up. We had been through so much together that I wondered if she were having a near-death experience and would soon arouse with another amazing adventure to tell.

She didn't move. I had never seen her so still. I could feel my heart pounding. I was sweating profusely. I could hear the steady drone of air circulating through the little vent above the door. I waited. Waited some more. I clasped her hand in mine and placed it on my forehead. I sort of tried to pray, but didn't know what to say. Then, I said the Lord's Prayer and asked that God's will be done, and somehow expected her to sit up. But, she didn't. She just lay there with a stillness that was totally resolute.

I felt a hand gently touch my shoulder, but no one was there. I stood up and stretched. As I faced the door it opened and the lady who had been at the reception desk walked in. She asked me if I were alright.

I was worried about the dog, Piper. I had left him in the car and had parked in an unauthorized space. As we walked down the hall, the lady motioned to an assistant and said they would call security and take care of it. It had seemed like just a few minutes, but I was told I had been with her for well over an hour and the staff was becoming concerned.

They gave me a glass of water. I signed some more papers and was given her personal belongings. They wanted an autopsy. I told them I really didn't like the idea, but I understood that they needed to conduct one. I selected a funeral home and was led outside. I took the dog for a walk, returned to the car, and went home. Alone.

As I walked up to the garage door I saw a large brown package. It had just been delivered via United Parcel Service. Susan had surprised me with a set of imported Glengary McLeod bagpipes, complete with all accessories. Somehow it seemed like the universe had traded me a set of pipes for my wife. I closed up the box and took it in the house.

I sat for awhile, then called my son and my closest friend. I told them I needed them to come to the house; it was important. They came immediately.

I took them outside next to the sweat lodge, between the two trees. I told them the events of my day. Then I said, "Our Priestess is gone. Susan died this morning."

All three of us stood in silence. My friend said he was shocked and my son gave me a hug. In a little while I said I wanted to be alone. They left. I went into the house and called my daughter. I told her, "We have lost all of them." I told her I needed her to come home.

The next day my son and I made arrangements for a simple memorial service. My daughter showed up a little later with her organizational magic and assumed control of the many details. The autopsy indicated that Suzy had died as the result of heart failure. She was a bit overweight, but this was totally unexpected. She had always expressed a preference for cremation. I remember walking slowly along, gazing at a display of urns and boxes. I was to select something that would contain her ashes.

As I was about to make my selection I suddenly felt her presence behind me. She clearly indicated "Yes, that one." It was a simple wooden box that had caught my eye just a moment before her communication. Susan knew what a hard time I can have making decisions about such things.

There was no doubt in my mind that she was present, and making it clear that the container would definitely be her choice. Her energy was powerful. She wanted to make things easier for me; to bring comfort through the knowledge that she was still present.

Our children put together a collection of several pictures from her life and artistically arranged them for a display. As I stood there staring at the pictures, I suddenly felt Susan rush by and comment, "Hey, I was some hot chick back then!" As she said it, I found myself repeating her message out loud. A family friend immediately knew it was Susan.

She was trying to be cheerful and upbeat. I think the effort at cheerfulness was as much for herself as it was for me. She seemed very curious and fascinated with the friends and family who had gathered and was enjoying watching and listening.

The memorial service was simple, but much more than I had expected. I was surprised at the number of people who attended. It was perhaps mostly due to my daughter's efforts. Several people, including myself provided the eulogy, along with a minister who was selected for the occasion. As would be expected, there were many fond memories of her.

All seemed taken by surprise. It had been sudden and unexpected. I kept saying it over and over. But another part of me was reluctantly realizing that this had been in the making for many months. Conscious realization was simply withheld from me. Now, all memories of the preparations that were obviously being made began to pour forth.

The family formed a line where those who wished could express their condolences. As they filed out, Susan was with me once more. One of her friends expressed concern that there had been some unresolved misunderstandings. Susan immediately spoke through me and assured the lady that all was well.

After the service, we brought the flowers to the grove under the willow trees. My daughter arranged flowers around the edge of our Nordic sweat lodge. We wandered about the area; feeling the moment, allowing ourselves to savor and reaffirm just how precious are our lives.

Again, Susan presented herself to me and offered a reassuring compliment to her son-in-law. Not quite being familiar with or schooled in such goings on, he wasn't sure he wanted to go there. But, he got the message, just the same.

It took several days for me to realize just how close the contact was that I was having with her. Through the intensity of the ordeal of her passing, I had somehow lost perspective. It took awhile to realize that what I was experiencing was quite extraordinary. Yet, it was feeling so matter of fact. One might be inclined to presume that I was merely experiencing the derangement of a bereaved spouse. But time and experience gave me the knowledge that this was not the case.

Several times she came near to me and would say over and over "See how it works. See how it works." She wanted me to experience and know what it was like to communicate with someone on the other side of the veil. Over and over, she wanted to assure me that all was well.

Sometimes I could sense that she would be standing near me, or by the wood stove in the living room. On several of those occasions, the dog would come in the room. He would alert and stare into space at the exact location where I too sensed her presence.

We had sometimes quarreled over vitamin and mineral supplements. Since the Source was always making suggestions and adjustments, Susan was the one who put together packets for us. The last few months she stopped. She said I should keep taking them. However, having relied on her for so long, I didn't know what to take. She wrote out a basic list and attached it to the cupboard door, explaining, "The Source says start with this and use your own intuition." I now realized she had not been taking the supplements for several months because she knew she no longer needed them.

Through the years she had always had court transcripts waiting to be completed. There were always billings that had been sent out to clients, waiting to be paid. I discovered that in the last days all of her transcripts had been completed, and payment had been received or was in the mail.

Several weeks before, she told her most active court reporters that she would no longer be available for court transcribing.

I remembered that, years before, the Source had expressed the idea that "the chances would be great that the soul (Susan) would withdraw once she had accomplished her mission."

Although all the signs of her passing had been there, right before me, I was somehow not allowed to put it all together. Perhaps it was best I didn't know.

She knew it was her time to leave. She left in the way she wanted. Hathrell had taken her safely to a quiet place where she would be discovered and tended to, without fanfare. It was the way that she wanted it.

One evening, I found myself very distraught; missing her and wondering what would come next in my life. As I sat in the darkened stillness, I abruptly felt her presence and briefly saw her image—actually kneeling before me, placing her hand on mine. With great compassion she explained, "I am right here. I will be with you for as long as you need me. All is well."

On another occasion she counseled, "If you wish, you could decide to come with me, but it is best if you stay. There are things you may yet accomplish which will be of great benefit to you and to those you meet." She affirmed that this was part of the reason that she had gone to provide me with different opportunities.

As time progressed, episodes of her presence became much less intense and occurred less often. On occasion, it seems she still looks in on me to see how things have progressed since her passing, but the connection is much more sublte, almost delegated to mere memory.

She had left my life almost as abruptly as she had come. At this point, we have both moved on, but we both remember.

Now a whole new life of adventure is unfolding.

The next year, I traveled to the Celtic festival at Estes Park in Colorado.

Eventually, I made pilgrimage to my ancestral home in Scotland. There, I escorted my chief, playing a solo of "Highland Cathedral" on my wee chanter, as a member of her procession moving up the path to the ancient pele tower. We were comemorating and celebrating the 900th year, of the acquisition of her lands through William the Conquerer.

Perhaps someday, you will hear my distant piping from out of the dawn of morning, or at the edge of evening's twilight; perhaps somewhere up high, perched upon a sacred mountain.

Perhaps someday, I shall meet you within the domain of Scotland's Ben Nevis, that grand promontory, replete with so much hystory and mystery.

Perhaps Jeb will nod and tip his hat as he rides by, beholdin' to none; but still in quest of his beloved ...

But all that is yet another story; just one more little story of the many stories—all woven together into the tapestry of the one big story that evolves into the magic that is our human sojourn.

Epilogue

When the funeral director presented her ashes, there were two containers; a big one and a little one. He explained this was highly unusual but sometimes does happen. After the first thick plastic bag was filled, there were three or four handfuls left over which were placed in a second, smaller bag. Each was sealed with the appropriately attached identification tags. Odd though it may have been, it felt quite natural for it seemed that metaphorically we had the ashes of both my beloved and of the little priestess. As had been one of Susan's musings, her ashes were released without ceremony into a river where they might eventually return to the sea.

It was late fall. The green on the mountainsides had first turned from green to yellow. What remained was mostly red and gold. The once emerald grass was becoming brown and brittle. A light, delicate rain had been intermittently misting through much of the day. In the high country, a sprinkling of snow across the granite peaks heralded another encroaching winter. Though the intermittent sun was still warm, the winds were icy cold and seemed to be accompanied by a soulful sighing. The trail had been wet and muddy. I was on pilgrimage to release the second bundle of ashes.

Near the headwaters of Bear Creek near Telluride is a small waterfall with a dark, cubed-shaped monolith of granite that is the size of a small cabin. It sits near a pool of slowly churning, crystal clear water, fed by a nearby waterfall. I crafted a small fire within the monolith's shadow while listening to the rushing of the water. After gently massaging numbed hands and fingers over warm, crackling coals, I sat cross-legged—suspended for awhile within the great silence.

The Source had claimed that the area around the cubed boulder was sometimes a portal between this world and the next. It was a place through which the dead might be released from earthly attachments and soar into the heavenly realms. It was also explained that it was a place through which spirits from other dimensions could visit the earth. Sometimes, through this portal it was even possible for those present in earthly bodies to visit other realms.

It seemed an appropriate place to release the remainder of the ashes: the remains representing Sho Ahd Shahanna Bhyong Mahadin. Praying and chanting, I thought about my many years with her as I methodically sprinkled the ashes into the waters, a little at a time until the little bag was empty at last.

As I lingered, I began to feel an inner whirling and shaking, as if some inner body was starting to spin and wobble. After a time, it dissipated. I rose and walked slowly down the slippery path towards the valley floor from which I had come.

When I reached the juncture of the stream flowing into the San Miguel River, I turned to gaze back up into the canyon. The gentle mist-filled rain was beginning to lift as a few remaining rays of sun streamed though the valley. High in the heavens, right over the place where I had left the ashes, were three perfect rainbows. I watched in quiet awe at such beauty and marveled at the timing. I remembered thinking that it was a good coincidence even if it had nothing to do with my ceremony of mourning and celebration.

No sooner had I completed the thought then an explosive lighting bolt lit up the ravine with a thunderous clap that was so strong it shook the trees, releasing some lingering leaves that cascaded haphazardly to the ground. Somewhere in my mind, I once again heard the words that the Source had spoken several times before, "Lest ye doubt."

In silence, I quietly retraced my steps to the car and returned home. Late that evening, after a long, hot bath, I lit the little candle in the meditation room and pulled the old woolen blanket tightly around my shoulders. Settling into the stillness, the strange swirling sensations I had experienced earlier that day began to return. There was tingling throughout my body; then a strong, pulling and drawing sensation began to surround me and radiated with a sort of tugging or pulling through the top of my head.

After a period of unconsciousness, I began to feel another body, slight, slender and young. I looked up to see hordes of bronze-skinned people dancing and singing with great joy. They were dressed in ornate garments, some with intricately colored robes graced with many varieties of feathers. The colors, feathers, and general fanfare were incredibly mesmerizing.

Surveying the scene, I realized I was sitting with a number of officials placed high atop an artificial stone promontory that may have been over a hundred feet high. I looked from side to side. It seemed I should be able to recognize the people around me, but I couldn't quite grasp who they were and why they felt so familiar.

An incredibly strong presence prodded my incredulous mind, challenging me to recall that this was Labhar, brother of the child priestess. He was such a proud young man, so focused and resolute. I was awed by his sense of determination and commitment.

I was there, with him, in his body; seeing through his eyes; thinking his thoughts; feeling his emotions. It was me, in a far and distant land, in a far and distant time.

Below, across an undulating mass of dancing celebrants, was a sort of cobblestone paved corridor lined with people moving around seven circles of seven drums, all laid out around a circular course in the plaza below. There was an increased flurry of movement and excitement as a procession was seen coming through the crowd like a ship slowly lumbering through water. In the center, was a large, meticulously adorned sedan chair covered with a golden-colored canopy. It was carried by twelve young men who were accompanied by twelve young women. There were several wind instruments or flutes of some kind playing along with the deep, resonant throbbing of the drums. It was a day of much fanfare, with the multitude harmoniously chanting and joyously dancing; all in unison.

Then, from out of the ocean of humanity, emerged a young woman adorned with gold, silver, and a huge headdress of bright yellow feathers that gracefully swayed as she walked. She had abandoned the ornate sedan chair that rested upon the platform that was now being carried several yards behind her. She was accompanied by two watchful attendants, one at each side, both looking fierce and menacing.

The party I was seated with stood and began to climb downward to meet her, navigating a long a series of brightly colored stone steps. She was mesmerizing.

Once again, I was being captured by incredible eyes. It was as if I was being invited to gaze deep into her soul. As the communion intensified, the recognition once again dawned within my heart and mind.

This was our little priestess: standing forth, fully grown. It was her coronation day as the High Priestess of the people of Mokhi Maha. We once more greeted and affirmed each other through the veil of time, travail, and victory.

It was Labhar seeing the triumph of his little sister. It was me, seeing my Susan once more.

She had persevered. The Source was with her; she was full of wisdom and compassion. She had stepped down from her carriage, gracefully walking through the crowd, offering gifts and blessings to the assembled devotees as she made the journey around the circle. The Priestess then led us back up the stairway to the top of the promontory where she accepted her appointment.

Hathrell's voice boomed in my head, announcing, "Good and faithful servant, it is done."

I was there, with her, in her Mokhi Maya. She had made it.

I was wrapped in a shroud of palpable bliss as the vision disassembled and faded. I opened my eyes and sat quietly in the darkened room, lit only by a flickering flame of a single candle.

I sat for the longest time, in quiet humility. Later, I slowly slid in between the soft, cool layers of the new feather bedding that Susan had purchased for me, and drifted off into a deep and nourishing sleep.

The next day, a whole new way of life, full of new challenges and adventure would be waiting … .

To the Children of the Light

Remember

Remember always that you are on quest. It is the perseverance, the faith, the service, the devotion to the life purpose by which you are measured.

REMEMBER that no one can walk your path for you. It is the ultimate responsibility to self, the reason for which you exist—your personal revelation, the epic journey that completes the circle of soul experience.

REMEMBER that all aspects of self are on the path of transformation. You must not deny those qualities which you judge to be negative; that is where the true work remains.

REMEMBER to reaffirm, evaluate, and serve your commitment on a frequent and regular basis. Remember that you are in a process of self-discovery. Know that it is the grace of God that you are not revealed to self all at once.

REMEMBER that as each layer of self-denial is removed, you must reassess, reaffirm, rededicate self, for your perspective and awareness will continually broaden and new potentials will be realized.

REMEMBER that you are a spiritual warrior, and that you live in a time when you must demand your birthright and reclaim the undiscovered land.

REMEMBER that "the land and the king are one."

REMEMBER that you are a pioneer, venturing into regions of self that have long been abandoned.

REMEMBER that this is the way home.

REMEMBER that when joyous revelations, visions, or openings of consciousness come, often expect a challenge, a seduction, an "opportunity" that will lead you astray. Begin to develop discernment, selectivity.

REMEMBER to treat self, all aspects of self with loving tenderness, patience, and compassion; as an infant that is learning to function.

REMEMBER to recognize self's weaknesses, particularly compartmentalization and stubborn pride, rather than true responsibility and service. The walls must come tumbling down for the light to come through.

REMEMBER that these self-imposed obstacles and pitfalls exist only in the conscious mind.

REMEMBER that each accomplishment, each overcoming, each time you look the dragon in the eye, each prayer given and received, makes the path easier for others and for self.

REMEMBER that the way to the inner sanctum, be it of the soul or the monastery, is to make self vulnerable to others.

REMEMBER to speak passionately of your yearnings, your failings, your insights, your path. Speak of your faults openly. Speak with the wisdom gained only through true self-awareness.

REMEMBER that pain, fear and confusion are the red flags that let you know that disharmony exists and questionable actions are being considered or pursued.

REMEMBER to go through the process of discussing and identifying the source of the problem. Is it fear of betrayal, of failing, of deprivation, things of the "lower" self? Is it the "higher" self crying out an impassioned plea to keep self on the straight path of commitment, to avoid another pitfall?

REMEMBER to keep a clear vision of your commitment. Do not allow others to tell you your goal is not possible, whoever they may be. This is where the stubborn willfulness and pride can be transformed into perseverance and devotion to path.

REMEMBER that you are born of the Sacred and Compassionate Heart of the Hawk Mother, you, the Eagle warrior, the bringer of light.

REMEMBER to continue to identify those concepts, those burdens, those expectations, those obligations placed on you by others, which have confused you, betrayed you, used you, abandoned you, bewildered you, and caused you to often betray yourself.

REMEMBER to see these others as yourself, with compassion, for they, too, are weak and seek fulfillment by wrong action.

REMEMBER to see how you have placed expectations, fulfillment, obligations, burdens, and blame upon others, and that they have in many ways betrayed you by not living up to your standards.

REMEMBER that you cannot walk another's path for them.

REMEMBER that it is balance within self that you seek.

REMEMBER that it is the perfection of the feminine nature within self that embodies the perfect "partner."

REMEMBER that it is unfair to expect another to fulfill that which can only be realized by self.

REMEMBER that no matter how many times you have fallen, again you have been lifted up to make the attempt again.

REMEMBER that the urgency of this period of existence for which you are now in the physical body occurs for only the fifth time since souls first manifested on this plane. This is a convergence of energies, a crossroads of unrealized potentials, a confirmation of commitments anciently made.

REMEMBER to listen to the inner voice of the soul, not the outer world of insane fantasies, distractions, and pitfalls.

REMEMBER forever "I never knew how empty was my soul until it was filled."

REMEMBER always who you really are.

REMEMBER that you are in the process of completing the circuit, of making the experience complete, of coming home.

REMEMBER, because "it is the failure of mankind that it forgets."

REMEMBER   REMEMBER   REMEMBER

Publisher's Note: This reading emerged from the Source at a time when those around the channel were becoming steeped in Arthurian movies, legend and mythology. It was offered after several prolonged episodes of personal instruction and guidance. The reading acknowledged a new beginning as a particular individual embarked on another stage of his life journey.

Later it was suggested that this could be used as a commemoration and remembering for all those who have been drawn to the readings "To the Children of the Light."

About the Author

This is the second book of a trilogy of the real life sagas of a modern American mystic. Dr. Hunter has spent much of his life in the exploration of both spiritual and religious practices. His experience as a householder, as well as a practicing Licensed Professional Counselor and Doctor of Psychology, give him some unique insights and observations into the search for things sacred.

At the time of this printing he spends most of his free time exploring the heritage of the American West and celebrating his Scottish ancestry. He continues to travel, write, and embrace the quest.